EXPLORING IRELAND'S WILD ATLANTIC WAY

Exploring Ireland's Wild Atlantic Way

A Motorcycle Odyssey

Eugene O'Loughlin

The Liffey Press

Published by
The Liffey Press Ltd
Raheny Shopping Centre, Second Floor
Raheny, Dublin 5, Ireland
www.theliffeypress.com

A catalogue record of this book is
available from the British Library.

ISBN 978-1-908308-55-9

Printed in Spain by GraphyCems

CONTENTS

Acknowledgements

Many people provided help and support throughout the year and a half it took me to ride and write about the Wild Atlantic Way. First, many thanks to Mick Doherty and Declan Weafer of Motorcycle City in Dublin who for 11 years have been servicing and fixing my Harley-Davidson, and who got it ready for my journey. My daughter Claire proof read early drafts of this book and provided invaluable advice on grammar and tone to which I hope I have paid attention. Yvan Vansevenant helped in my research of several people and locations, and I am also grateful to Joe O'Loughlin (no relation) of County Fermanagh for his help in researching the O'Loughlin family in County Clare.

Without exception I was made welcome wherever I went. To the many people in bed & breakfasts, pubs, cafés, restaurants, tourist offices, museums, interpretative centres, and to those who live on the Wild Atlantic Way, I express my heartfelt thanks for the various stories, directions, places to stay, and of course food and drink. In particular, I would like to thank Dorothy Bourke, and Mark and Antoinette Bourke for their hospitality in County Mayo. The following people also helped me in many small and large ways: Joe O'Loughlin, Kathleen Kelleher, Leo Casey, Carissa Casey, Stephan Weibelzahl, Pat Cleere, Sheila O'Donnell, Gráinne Foley, and Paddy Mathews (Fáilte Ireland). Thanks also to Peter Murtagh and Pól Ó Conghaile for providing some kind words for the back cover.

Acknowledgements

To David Givens of The Liffey Press I owe a great debt. He helped me to turn my rambling prose, with a heavy dose of blunt and forth-right advice, into the pages that make up this book. Finally, I'd like to thank my family for their love and support, especially when I seemed to be constantly in front of a computer screen. To my Mum Phil and Dad Joe, you taught me always to learn and to be constantly curious, and for that I will be always grateful. To my daughters Claire, Kate, and Vicki, thank you for supporting me and putting up with a Dad who likes big motorbikes. Lastly, I could not have done this without the support and love of my wife Roma, who has always stood by me and helped me to follow my dreams. Still mad about you.

Dedicated with all my love to Roma, Claire, Kate, and Vicki

PROLOGUE

There is something about looking at a map with a set route and thinking, 'I can do that'. Curiosity makes me wonder about the sights to see, the people to meet, and things to do and discover at each place of interest along the route. A sense of adventure gripped me when I first studied the Wild Atlantic Way and there was only one thing on my mind: this map demanded that I ride the entire route on my motor-cycle from Kinsale in the south to Inishowen in the north.

I live in Dublin on the east coast of Ireland and the Wild Atlantic Way runs through many parts of the western side of the island of Ire-land that I had never been to. The Wild Atlantic Way was developed by Fáilte Ireland to provide, at over 2,500 kilometres, the longest defined coastal driving route in the world along the rugged, unspoilt and un-tamed western coast of Ireland. The route passes through many well-known and iconic tourist attractions such as the Cliffs of Moher and the Ring of Kerry, but it also passes through some of the less well-known places of interest such as Toe Head in County Cork and Blacksod Bay in County Mayo. There are over 150 Discovery Points along the way which are well signposted by Fáilte Ireland. Of course there are hundreds more points of discovery along and within short distances of the route ready and waiting to tempt you off the Wild Atlantic Way. That's the wonderful thing about the Wild Atlantic Way – you can make it your own personal odyssey. All you have to do is to get on the road and keep the Atlantic Ocean to one side. So whatever your interest – old castles, rock formations, sea views, narrow winding roads, long beaches, meeting people, or good food – there is something for everybody on the Wild Atlantic Way.

My choice of vehicle is my 2003 Harley-Davidson Heritage Softail Classic motorcycle. I have been riding motorcycles since I was 19 years old and today in my mid-fifties I still get the same thrill every time I start up the bike as I did when I first experienced the open road on two wheels. I have been through several wonderful journeys on my bike through Western Europe and America, but this time I looked to my own country for my next adventure. I decided to ride the Wild Atlantic Way in one go over ten days, but I deliberately set out with no formal plan in mind. My only rules were to follow the signs for coast roads, keep the sea to my left, and to ride.

So I set out from Dublin to Kinsale to begin the Wild Atlantic Way; this would be my motorcycle odyssey.

1

WEST CORK – A PLACE APART

They say that West Cork is 'A Place Apart', so there could be no better starting point for me to set out on my journey around the Wild Atlantic Way than the picturesque fishing port of Kinsale. It is often referred to as the Gourmet Capital of Ireland as it features many restaurants, cafés and pubs to suit all tastes. Following the three hour ride from my home in Dublin, I parked the bike on the waterfront and took some time to stroll around the narrow winding streets. Kinsale is a beautiful town in a wonderful setting that needs some time to explore; you could spend all day here and feel yourself relaxing by the minute.

One of Kinsale's best known visitor attractions is Charles Fort on the eastern side of the harbour. It is one of the finest surviving examples of a seventeenth century star-shaped fort, so in what was to be one of many detours from the Wild Atlantic Way I decided to check it out. Much of the original fort construction, which started in 1678, remains today. It is named after King Charles II of England and its star shape was specifically designed to resist attack by cannon. Across the harbour is the older James Fort, built in 1607 and named after King James I. Charles Fort provided protection for the natural harbour of Kinsale and continued in use by the British army until 1922. The bare walls and roofless buildings have stood like this since it was burned down during the Irish Civil War. It is now a National Monument of Ireland. Even though it is a pity to see so many ruined buildings, the site

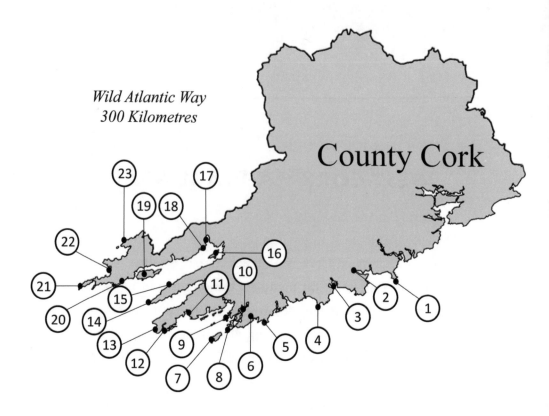

Wild Atlantic Way
300 Kilometres

County Cork

Wild Atlantic Way – West Cork Discovery Points

1. Kinsale Head	2. Timoleague Abbey	3. Inchydoney Island
4. Galley Head	5. Toe Head Bay	6. Lough Hyne
7. Clear Island	8. Sherkin Island	9. Heir Island
10. Inish Beg	11. Toormore Bay	12. Barley Cove
13. Mizen Head	14. Sheep's Head	15. Seefin Viewpoint
16. Whiddy Island	17. Garnish Island	18. Whiddy Island View
19. Bear Island	20. Fairhead Viewpoint	21. Dursey Island
22. Ballydonegan Viewpoint	23. Kenmare River View	

is maintained in immaculate condition by the Office of Public Works (OPW) and it is open all year round. The fort provides wonderful views across to Kinsale, and after about 20 minutes walking around the ruined buildings I set off for the other side of the harbour.

I left Kinsale to ride into an area known as De Courcey Country. The area got this name in the twelfth century, when a Norman knight called Milo de Cogan received this land as a gift from Henry II of England. His daughter Margaret married Myles De Courcey in 1223 who received this beautiful land as a dowry and he then modestly named the area after himself. One of De Courcey Country's best known landmarks is the Old Head of Kinsale which is about 13 kilometres to the southwest of Kinsale. As I got close to Old Head I stopped at the Lusitania Memorial which is also a super viewing point to see the Old Head. The *Lusitania* was infamously sunk on the afternoon of 7 May 1915 when it was torpedoed by a German U-Boat about 16 kilometres south of Old Head. It sank in just 18 minutes with a loss of over 1,000 lives. I wondered if anyone was standing on this very spot looking out to sea on that fateful day to witness this great tragedy. There is a rather forbidding gate at the entrance to the golf club that occupies the Old Head, and I decide not to try to bluff my way out to the Old Head Lighthouse pretending to play golf. The Old Head peninsula is beautifully flat and has great views out to sea on both sides. I turned away from one of the most famous landmarks in Ireland and rode on deeper into West Cork.

By now it was late afternoon and I took a quick detour inland to Ballinspittle to get some petrol and to check out the village made famous in 1985 by the moving statue of Our Lady. The grotto where the statue is located has plenty of room for worshippers and curious bikers. It was very quiet there today; I was the only person there. I parked my bike right in front of the grotto, in case Our Lady fancied a ride on a Harley-Davidson. Our Lady did not move, but I did, onwards.

Continuing on to Timoleague, I stopped at the huge ruin of a Friary founded by the Franciscans in the year 1240. This is a very impressive

Kinsale Harbour
(photo by Kathleen Kelleher)

building that dominates the town. A timeline sign on the wall of the friary tells us that it was burned down in 1642 by 'Cromwellian soldiers'. I think that this is one crime in Ireland that Oliver Cromwell is not guilty of as he did not set foot in Ireland until 1649. While getting ready to get back on board my bike I was approached by an Australian tourist couple who had parked their car next to it. They stood admiring the bike and asking me questions about the size of the engine and how fast it would go. The guy told me he once had a bike when he was younger and that he really wanted to get one again, but 'hadn't got around' to it; I get this a lot.

A short distance from Timoleague just off the Wild Atlantic Way is the town of Courtmacsherry where I decided to end the day. On the way I stopped at the ruins of a Cistercian Abbey at Abbeymahon. These ruins date from the twelfth century and there is not much left to see of what was once undoubtedly a fine abbey. The land around and inside the ruins has been used as a very small cemetery and one notable grave shows a First World War headstone over the remains of stoker Denis Driscoll who, the gravestone tells us, served on *HMS Venerable* during the war. He died in 1919, though the gravestone looks very new. It is good to see that the Irish dead from World War I are now being remembered in this way, even in this remote location.

The approach to Courtmacsherry is glorious, especially on a lovely evening like today. The road into the village runs right on the edge of Courtmacsherry Bay, and in the early evening sunshine it felt like I was riding into a film set. I booked into the excellent old-style Travara Lodge guesthouse, decided to wander about, and stopped for a pint of Murphy's stout in the Pier Harbour bar where I was also able to avail of free WiFi. I sat in the window overlooking the bay and got into conversation with a gadget-laden Englishman about technology and broadband reach in more remote areas like Courtmacsherry. The speed here was very good, and we compared my iPad and his iPhone like two boys comparing who had dug up the biggest worm. For dinner I had a super

Timoleague Abbey

fish pie in the Lifeboat Bar, which was right beside my accommodation for the evening. Before going to bed, I decided to go for a walk and ended up in the peaceful Courtmacsherry Hotel to watch the end of the day from the comfortable position of a bar stool. I had come a long way since setting out from Dublin in the morning and after checking that my bike was securely locked I slept like someone who had just ridden a bike all day.

Cork is the largest county in Ireland and I certainly found that out today in that I started at 9.30 in the morning from Courtmacsherry and at 19.30 arrived in Bantry, still in County Cork. It is a county that I have discovered has a spectacular coast line, and I certainly had a great

ride around the ins and outs of the Cork coast. The day started off with a big breakfast courtesy of the Travara Lodge. I shared a table with a man from England called Danny who had been at his brother's funeral the previous day. He told me he was originally from Cork and that it was his first visit 'home' in many years. We discussed the differences between funerals in Ireland and England, and Danny was amazed that so many people turned up for his brother's funeral. Visibly upset at the sad occasion that had caused him to return to Ireland, he commented that his own funeral in England would be attended by many fewer people. He liked the way that Irish people mourned their dead, and I detected a little jealously of the fine attendance at his brother's last event.

If you have the time there is a nice detour from the Wild Atlantic Way where you can travel the 42.5 kilometre Seven Heads Walkway which starts and ends in Timoleague. It was difficult to tell from my maps which headlands made up the Seven Heads. In the sea off the coast here is the Kinsale Head Gas Field. One of the satellite fields, discovered in 2003, is also known as the Seven Heads Gas field. Seven Heads marks the beginning of the eastern side of Clonakilty Bay, which is divided up into many smaller bays and coves. From the tiny village of Ring to Clonakilty there is a small, but super road to ride all the way along the bay, with only a small wall to keep the sea back from the road. The views to Inchydoney Island, which is not really an island, across the bay, make this one of the best coastal rides in West Cork.

Evening in Courtmacsherry

Waiting for crossing cows near Clonakilty

Clonakilty is a beautiful town made famous (for me) by some fantastic sausages and black pudding, but it is much more than this. As with many other towns on my route, I wish I could have spent more time here. The town was bedecked in colour as it was hosting the 'Random Acts of Kindness' festival. This was set up in the aftermath of heavy flooding in the town in early 2012. Its message is: 'Cut the misery. Spread the positivity.' I stopped briefly to admire the statue of Michael Collins in Emmet Square. Collins lived here briefly with his sister Margaret from 1904 to 1906. The statue was unveiled in 2002 on the 80th anniversary of his death by the actor Liam Neeson, who played the part of this Irish hero in the movie *Michael Collins*. Curiously, for such a well-known Irish patriot, this was also the first statue of him ever erected. While riding through the town centre I noticed a sign for 'The Michael Collins Centre', and as it was still early morning I decided to take a short detour from the coast roads and head inland to check it out. The centre provides a detailed exhibition on the life and times of Collins, and even has a replica of the ambush site where he died. You'll need at least an hour to take in everything, but it is worth the effort if you want to find out more about Collins from the experts at the centre.

Leaving Clonakilty I headed for Galley Head via Inchydoney Island. I stopped to look over at the famous Inchydoney Island Lodge and Spa, which is set in a magnificent location overlooking the sea beside a wonderful beach. I stopped at the side of the road and noticed some small ponies in the field in front of me. My noisy bike had not scared them off and I enjoyed looking at these beautiful creatures in this quiet location. Be warned, though: the roads in this region are very poor as a result of flood damage.

Ponies at Inchydoney

At Galley Head there is a lighthouse and ancient walls of an old Norman stronghold called Dún Deidi. The lighthouse was built in 1875 and is reputedly one of the most powerful in Europe. Just past Galley Head is a wonderful beach called the Long Strand, with some magnificent dunes behind it. I also noticed here an unusually shaped small lake, called Kilkern Lake, near Castlefreke; it looked similar to a Facebook thumbs-up 'Like' symbol. By now I was looking out over Rosscarbery Bay where the coastline seemed to stretch forever. It was now mid-morning and time for a break. I stopped in the quiet village of Rosscarbery for a coffee and the largest slice of the most delicious carrot cake ever at the Pilgrim's Rest café. I took the opportunity to check my maps and see what was up ahead. As I saw names of places like Union Hall, Castletownshend, Baltimore and Ballydehob, I knew that I was in for a treat in the most picturesque part of West Cork.

Long Strand beach

Drombeg Stone Circle

Close to Rosscarbery on the way to Glandore I stopped at the Drombeg Stone Circle. Even though it was marked on my map, it was not that easy to find on the twisty roads and I had to stop several times to check the map, and even looked up Google Maps satellite view to see if I could spot a stone circle in this area. But once I found it down an even twistier lane, it was worth the effort to locate it. An OPW sign tells us that the stone circle dates from the Bronze Age (1100–800 B.C.), and was associated with human burial. The 17 stones are set in such a way that on the winter solstice the main axis of the circle point is aligned with the setting sun. A few metres away from the stone circle is a cooking pit called a *fulacht fiadh* where Bronze Age chefs boiled water for cooking with stones heated in a fire. During excavations here in 1957, archaeologists conducted an experiment which showed that 70 gallons (318 litres) of cold water could be brought to the boil in just 18 minutes. The multi-purpose *fulacht fiadh* was also used for bathing and even for brewing.

I continued on to the nearby village of Glandore which is located in a beautiful setting with a tiny harbour which was full of small boats and

View from Glandore towards Union Hall

people preparing to go out sailing as I passed. The bay here is called Glandore Harbour and it is a very pleasant ride up one side and down the other. Across the middle of the harbour is the narrow Poulgorm Bridge, which is only wide enough for one car to pass at a time. This bridge was used by David Puttnam in his 1994 film *War of the Buttons*, where two gangs of boys were separated by a white line on the bridge.

The fishing village of Union Hall lies on the western side of Glandore Harbour. At the entrance to the village is a new monument with a huge anchor which was recovered from the sea near here in 1999. The impressive black anchor is just over 7 metres in height and weighs 5 tonnes. It is thought to date from the early 1700s and belonged to an unknown French ship. Like many other fishing villages, Union Hall has had its share of tragedy. Early in 2012 five fishermen, including three

Union Hall

from Egypt, were drowned when a trawler called the *Tit Bonhomme* sank just off the coast here. The desperate and tragic search for the bodies of the men went on for several weeks and was headline news for a long time while the local community waited for the sea to yield up the dead. Just two days after I passed through here a memorial was erected to the five men in the village, and later in the year the community was presented with a People of the Year Award. Union Hall is a relatively new village in that it is believed to have been founded in the early nineteenth century. The name is thought to be based on the 1801 Act of Union between Great Britain and Ireland. Close by is the hilly village of Castletownshend, named after the Townsend family that have lived there since about 1640. The steep main street leads down to a harbour and a castle where the Townsends lived. On the other side of the harbour is a small spit of land called The League. It was here during the Great Famine that several whales were beached and provided much needed relief for the starving people of the area. While the sea takes, it also gives up its bounty when needed.

Leaving Castletownshend I soon spotted a sign for the curiously named Toe Head. I stopped to look at my map to see what this landmark could be, and it was easy to see how this almost foot-shaped headland got its name. Unfortunately, I will remember it both for its beauty and my first accident of my trip. After a few kilometres of some very narrow roads going nowhere, I began to think that I had made a wrong turn. I stopped to check my position on my iPhone, but there was no signal. I pulled into the driveway of a bungalow and tried to turn around very slowly at the sloped entrance. However, I could not hold the bike up and it fell over on its side, the first time this ever happened to me. Fortunately, I was able to step away in time. I had never seen the underside of my bike before. I noted how dirty it was, and wondered how on earth I was going to get this 400 kilogramme lump of iron back on two wheels. Fortunately, the owners of the house, Brian and Eileen, came out to my assistance and we got the bike upright again. They were so kind to me offering tea as well as helping me to get the

*Gortacrossig Lookout Tower
at Toe Head*

Lough Hyne

bike back on two wheels. They were Dubliners who had moved to Cork
13 years ago, and they loved this fantastic quiet location where they
live. My pride was hurt, and I was also embarrassed at the dirty state of
the underside of my bike. Brian told me that I was indeed on the right
road to Toe Head and that I could make my way up to the Gortacrossig
Lookout Tower on the top of the hill overlooking the headland with
fantastic views. What he didn't tell me was that the 'road' would be
cleverly disguised as a dirt track and that it was totally unsuitable for
a Harley-Davidson. I crawled to the top expecting at any second for
the bike to fall over again, but when I got there I knew why Brian and
Eileen had moved here from Dublin. On top of the hill overlooking Toe
Head are the ruins of a small castle. I stopped to take some photos and
to drink in the scenery. I felt as though I was the only person on earth
in this peaceful setting. This peace was shattered in 1986 with the Kow-
loon Bridge disaster when the drifting super tanker crashed on to the
rocks near here. There were 2,000 tonnes of fuel and 160,000 tonnes
of steel on board. The resulting oil spill caused great coastal pollution

in the area, and the wreck still lies undersea where it is an attraction for scuba divers. Thankfully, the coast has recovered from this disaster.

Much chastened and still slightly shaken from my visit to Toe Head I aimed for the more peaceful surroundings of the Lough Hyne Marine Nature Reserve. This is a unique marine lake where the diversity of habitats and species in such a small area attracts biologists of all types. The lake has a narrow opening called The Rapids which goes out to the sea. In such a small lake there are shallow rocky areas as well as deep underwater cliffs. Lough Hyne is close to the picturesque fishing village of Baltimore where I stopped and parked my bike at an old style water pump across the road from Bushe's Bar where I had some delicious soup and sandwiches. This was also beside Dún na Séad castle, which is the given name for Baltimore in the Irish language. The castle was built in 1215, but fell into ruin after being taken over by Oliver Cromwell. It is now restored and is a favourite local tourist attraction. From Baltimore you can take ferries to the nearby Sherkin Island, Heir Island and Cape Clear. The ferries are mostly passenger only, which makes for a problem for bikers unless you have a safe and secure place to leave your bike and all your gear. The longest ferry trip is to Cape Clear which takes about 45 minutes.

About 5 kilometres outside of Baltimore on the road to Skibbereen is a turn to the left for the small island of Inishbeg, which is accessible via a beautiful walled bridge. The island is home to the Inish Beg Estate, which is a popular water sports destination, but is perhaps better known for its colourful gardens which were listed in the 100 best gardens in Ireland for the year 2011. Just a few metres past the road for Inishbeg I passed by a sign for the 'Grave of Canon Goodman' and wondered who he was and why he deserved a sign to himself. The sign points to a narrow lane and there was just enough space to park my bike at the gateway at the side of the road which leads to the ruined Creagh Church. Canon James Goodman's headstone records his death in 1896 and also states that he was a curate here from 1852 to 1858.

But Canon Goodman is known more than just as a curate in Creagh. He was a rector in Skibbereen (about 8 kilometres from his grave) for 29 years and collected a priceless legacy of over 2,000 Irish melodies whose manuscripts are now kept in the Library at Trinity College in Dublin. These songs were collected in the years after the Great Famine, and many would have certainly been lost but for his efforts. He was made Professor of Irish in Trinity in 1879, and from then until he died spent six months in Dublin and six months in this area. He was a well know piper in his day, and also a classical scholar. I rode into Skibbereen where I found a statue to Canon Goodman just inside the gate of the Abbeystrewry parish church which shows him playing the uilleann pipes. I sure would have liked to have met him and perhaps we could have sung a song or two.

Creagh Church near Baltimore

Back on the road I noticed another biker that I had seen a couple of times earlier in the day, and we waved at one another a few times. I had noticed that as I got further away from populated areas, as well as travelling on narrow roads, that there were fewer and fewer bikers to be seen. Motorcyclists have a habit on acknowledging each other on the road with a nod or a wave. Irish bikers have to be careful when waving. As we are a left-hand drive country, other traffic comes from the right, but it is natural to wave with the right hand. For a biker, the right hand's main purpose in life is to work the throttle, so we must remember to wave with the left hand, or else the bike will slow down. When riding in America, I was of course on the other side of the road and waving with the left hand was more natural. Also, there were many more Harley-Davidsons and I seemed to be waving at other bikers all the time. American bikers like to hold out their left hands in a low position with an open palm as if to give a 'low five'. In France I had noticed that some riders stuck their leg out as they passed me and I incorrectly assumed that they were insulting my Harley-Davidson and me in the fashion of a dog peeing against a lamppost. I later discovered that this was a signal for 'thanks', usually given when you allow another biker to pass.

The road from Skibbereen to Ballydehob was mostly inland from the coast, so I moved on a bit quicker as I was travelling on some quite good roads. I had intended to ride straight through Ballydehob, but I decided to stop briefly and ended up staying a bit longer in this historical town. Ballydehob is the home of Steve Redmond, who in 2012 became the first person in the world to complete the Ocean's Seven challenge, which is a group of seven long distance swims from all over the world: the Irish Channel between Scotland and Northern Ireland; the Cook Strait between the North and South islands in New Zealand; the Moloka'i Channel in Hawaii; the English Channel between Britain and France; the Catalina Channel in California; the Tsugaru Strait in Japan; and the Straits of Gibraltar between Spain and Morocco.

Ballydehob

They are very proud of Redmond here, and his Ocean's Seven challenge makes my Wild Atlantic Way journey look like a walk in the park. Maybe the locals will build a statue to him on the main street like they did for Danno O'Mahony who also hailed from Ballydehob and was 'Heavyweight All In World Wrestling Champion of the World 1935–1936', according to his statue. He was just 22 years old when he won the title in Boston. Sadly, Danno died in a traffic accident in 1950. Ballydehob was looking like a very interesting place and I decided to explore further in this charming town.

Close beside Danno's statue are new two plaques, one commemorating the *Titanic*, and the other a speech by Anna Parnell. Two local women, Bridget Driscoll and Annie Jane Jermyn, were among the passengers of the *Titanic* when it sank in 1912. These two, and a third woman, Mary Kelly from Westmeath, bought their tickets at the Ballydebob Shipping Agency for seven pounds and fifteen shillings. The tickets were numbered consecutively: 14311, 14312, and 14313. All three survived the disaster, escaping on the last lifeboat launched. Right beside the *Titanic* plaque is another marking a speech by Anna Parnell, a sister of Charles Stewart Parnell, who was founder and leader of the Ladies Land League. She spoke to a crowd of over 4,000 supporters here on 30 March 1881. In her speech she proclaimed Ballydehob as 'the grandest place in the world', and that the name Ballydehob was a 'fighting sound', which I'm sure got a great cheer from the crowd. Ballydehob is also the location for a fantastic 12 arches railway bridge which once was part of the railway line between Skibbereen and Schull. It was first put into use in 1886 and must have looked like one of the Wonders of the World to the people here at that time. The railway line closed in 1947, and I'm sure it was a fantastic sight to see a steam powered train cross over this bridge. Ballydehob is located on the wonderfully named Roaringwater Bay, which is the southernmost bay on mainland Ireland. Moving on I was now riding on the Mizen Head Peninsula, which was the first of five spectacular peninsulas in counties Cork and Kerry. By now it was late afternoon and I had to ride on to get this area explored before settling down for the evening.

On the road to Schull there are some spectacular rock formations on Mount Gabriel, which is to the right side of the road. On top of the mountain, and clearly visible on the journey to and from Mizen Head, are two radar domes which look like two large golf balls. These make up one of nine radar stations in Ireland which support the Air Traffic Control network. The slanted rock formation on the mountain side adds to the scenery giving it a rugged look. At one time copper was mined here, and some of the small tunnels used for mining are still preserved today. In a very busy Schull I made a brief stop to look out over Schull Harbour and to the islands beyond in Roaringwater Bay. The islands in this bay are called Carbery's 100 Isles, after the Barony of Carbery, and you can see one of the biggest, Clear Island, from here. Amid beautiful rocky scenery on all sides I continued on the coastal route around

Toormore Bay and got my first glimpse of the Fastnet Rock, clearly visible out to sea on this fine clear day. A lighthouse was first built on the rock in 1853, though the current one is the more iconic white lighthouse finished in 1904. I was interested to discover later that it is made up of 2,047 granite dovetailed blocks brought all the way from Cornwall in England. I had heard that Fastnet was often referred to as 'Ireland's Teardrop' as for many emigrants to the New World Ireland's most southerly building will have been the last part of Ireland they saw. The lighthouse marks the midpoint on the famous biannual Fastnet Race for yachts from the Isle of Wight, which round the lighthouse and head back to Plymouth, a distance of 1,126 kilometres. Though the seas are very calm today, this was not the case during the 1979 race when

Barley Cove

Mizen Head

a storm caused the deaths of 15 sailors. Close to the end of the Mizen Head peninsula is the village of Crookhaven, which was once the last port of call in Europe for shipping crossing the Atlantic Ocean. Nearby is one of the most picturesque beaches you will see at Barley Cove. It is also a European Union designated Special Area of Conservation as the sand dunes provide a diverse habitat for wildlife. The best views of Barley Cove are from the western side of the cove.

I finally arrived at the end of the peninsula to the most south westerly point in Ireland, Mizen Head. The low sun was lighting up the coast in beautiful picture postcard brightness. This rocky outcrop features a lighthouse and a Marconi radio signal station, plus a shop and restaurant. I bought a ticket in the Visitor Centre and set out to see what for me is one of Ireland's best kept secrets. There are paths and steps to show the way, but some of these paths are very steep. There is a new bridge over a large gorge that takes you out to a ship's bridge room and the signal station. It was almost closing time, so I did a quick tour around the museum. It was once manned continuously, but is now a museum showing how a Marconi system worked. I chatted to one of the museum staff who told me that aerials on top of the Head are still working and in use, but that much of what the signal station once existed for has now been replaced by satellite global positioning systems (GPS). I went up to the highest point and after catching my breath after so many steps I just looked around at the jagged rocky outcrops that dot the coast here. The low sun, and its reflection from the sea, made for a spectacular view, and made me wish I was good at photography so that I could capture it all. To the north was the Beara Peninsula and to the south I could still see the Fastnet Lighthouse. On my way to the exit I stopped at the Fastnet Lighthouse Centenary Stone Course which

Bridge on Mizen Head

The author on Mizen Head

shows a model of how the granite stones of the lighthouse are cleverly fixed together. While admiring this I was told by one of the museum staff that they were locking up, and I reluctantly left this unmissable treat.

I took the road on the northern side of the Mizen Head peninsula and enjoyed the views of Dunmanus Bay towards Sheep's Head on the other side of the bay. At Durrus I stopped to look at my map; left was towards Sheep's Head, and right was towards Bantry. I decided to continue on to Bantry and to return to this point in the morning as my backside was telling me that I really needed to get off the bike. I rode into Bantry and checked in to the Kylemore B&B on the Glengarriff Road, which was run by the chatty and welcoming Eilish. Bantry is home to many festivals and activities; the town buzzes during the summer with colour and people everywhere. Once settled in, I made my way downtown to the Wheel House Bar in the Bantry Bay Hotel where

Bantry

I availed of free WiFi and had a super Scampi dinner for just €9.00. It had been a long day since I had set out from Courtmacsherry and with great weather all day I certainly enjoyed myself in this part of West Cork. I had seen some of the most spectacular scenery that Ireland has to offer, but also had suffered an accident to remind me to pay attention to the road. Tomorrow would be my last day in Cork, but there was still much more to see and do.

Next morning at breakfast I met the landlady, Eilish, who was getting breakfast ready for her guests. She started singing the Willie Nelson song 'On the Road Again' to get us in the mood for touring. The Germans have a lovely word, *Ohrwurm* (ear worm), to describe a song that stays in your head even though you can't hear it. 'On the Road Again' was my *Ohrwurm* for the rest of the day!

Before leaving Bantry I rode down to the town centre and parked in Wolfe Tone Square for a look around. Theobald Wolfe Tone, who is often regarded as the father of Irish Republicanism, was one of the founding members of the United Irishmen who rebelled against British rule in 1798. Two years earlier, Tone was part of a French fleet of 43 ships and over 14,000 men that could not land in Bantry Bay because of storms. After eight days they sailed back to France; Tone had not set foot in Bantry. He is reputed to have said, 'We were near enough to toss a biscuit ashore'. Later, he was to die in a Dublin prison in 1798. In the middle of the square there is a fine statue of him looking out to Bantry Bay.

Two other items of interest in the square were a statue

St Brendan the Navigator

of St Brendan 'the Navigator' and a large anchor. St Brendan's statue is in front of Wolfe Tone and shows him in a Christ the Redeemer-like pose looking out to sea. He is reputed to have discovered America 800 years before Christopher Columbus. The anchor, which is behind the statue of Wolfe Tone, was recovered from the local bay and, according to an attached plaque, is from one of the French ships that sank during the 1796 storms. Bantry is full of history, but it was time for me to move on.

On a glorious morning I set out for the Sheep's Head peninsula. This meant travelling back to Durrus and continuing on from where I had left off yesterday. I rode along the coastal road with the Mizen Head peninsula to my left on the other side of Dunmanus Bay. Just outside Ahakista is a memorial to victims of the 1985 Air India disaster, when 329 people flying from Montréal to New Delhi in India died as a result of a mid-air explosion off the south west coast of Ireland. The garden is in a beautiful and peaceful setting, and is well worth the few moments it takes to stop and remember the victims. The garden features a sundial and a wall with a list of the names of those who died. A striking thing about this list is the number of people with the same surname; whole families were wiped out in a moment. After this sombre stop I moved on to Sheep's Head where at the end of the road there is a bit of a hike out to the lighthouse, but it is worth the effort as the views were spectacular, especially back towards Mizen Head. The views get better and better, and I can't get enough of this. There were not too many people about, but I was worried about the security of my bike so I walked quite quickly on the difficult path out to the Head. I hoped that

Air India Memorial in Akahista

Sheep's Head

potential thieves were not yet up at this hour of the morning. There is a small lake called Lough Akeen near the tip of the peninsula and beside it you can make out rows of furrows where potatoes were once grown. I could now also see the Beara Peninsula where I was heading to next. This place is so peaceful with not a sound to be heard other than a squawk from a passing seagull. I wished that I could just sit here and breathe in the cleanest air in Europe, but I reluctantly had to turn around and leave Sheep's Head behind.

I travelled back towards Bantry through Kilrohane. When the road reached the coast again I stopped close to the small Seefin mountain to gaze upon Bantry Bay and the Beara Peninsula on the other side. From here the road runs right along the coast until you reach Whiddy Island. This island is probably best known for the huge Gulf Oil ter-

Glengarriff

minal located there, and you can get a short ferry trip to see the island. In the last few months of World War I there was a small United States sea plane air station based at the island, though little remains of this base today.

On to the Beara Peninsula, where I stopped in Glengarriff for a coffee at Harrington's Bar. It was very pleasant to sit outside this bar in the sun and I chatted to a man called Douglas from Macroom about – what else? – the weather. Here the Caha Mountains almost reach the sea at Glengarriff Harbour where there are lots of small islands, including Garnish Island which features a world renowned garden which specialises in rare plants from all over the globe. Glengarriff Woods are part of a Nature Reserve, and there are trees everywhere around here. This location marks the start of the 195 kilometre Ring of Beara tourist trail, and I set out in glorious sunshine on this spectacularly scenic route. With Bantry Bay and views back to Whiddy Island to my left, and rocky hills and mountains to my right, I was certainly enjoying what must be one of the best motorcycle rides in Ireland. It is almost impossible not to stop and drink in the scenery.

At Castletown Bearhaven I stopped again to look out towards Bear Island, and to take a look at my map. I noticed that there was a Stone Circle marked a short distance away inland, so I decided to take a small detour from the coast road to see what our Bronze Age ancestors were up to 3,000 years ago in this beautiful area. The Derreenataggart Stone Circle is one of many such circles around Ireland. I did not know this, but a sign at the location tells us that these circles were always made up of an uneven number of standing stones. Here there are twelve surviving stones; the original circle is thought to have consisted of fifteen stones.

Dursey Island marks the end of the Beara Peninsula. Like Sheep's Head earlier in the day, this was a very quiet location and I felt that I was disturbing the peace with my loud exhaust pipes as I parked at the

Dursey Island

end of the road. There were quite a few people about to see the cable car link to Dursey Island, which is the only one of its type in Ireland and has been operating here since 1969. There's no bridge to the island, and the creaking cable car was for passengers only (though sheep and cattle are sometimes also carried on it), so unfortunately I did not go out to the island. The views are once again spectacular and I can now see the Ring of Kerry to the north. As I get back on my bike I notice two roads signs, one for New York, which is 4,950 kilometres away, and one for Moscow, which is 3,883 kilometres in the opposite direction. I never felt as far away from either city as I did here today. It was with a heavy heart that I left the end of the Beara Peninsula in still glorious sunshine. By now it was mid-afternoon and I started to think about lunch. Before setting off I looked at my map again and decided on the nearby village

Ring of Kerry near Dursey Island

of Allihies as a likely place to try. On the way to Allihies I made two short stops. The first was at the Loughane More Ring Fort, which is one of over 45,000 such ring forts identified in Ireland. According to Geograph Ireland, one theory is that they were used from 500–1,000 AD to safeguard livestock. Following this, I noticed just before the village of Allihies a sign pointing to a Children of Lir Mystical Site. Every child growing up in Ireland knows the legend of the Children of Lir who were transformed into swans for 900 years by their jealous step-mother. At the site a sign tells us that after 900 years they heard a bell being rung by a monk in Allihies, came ashore near here and immediately were turned into humans again. Legend has it that they are buried under the large white boulders that you can see here. Some small change is left on the boulders as an offering to the children.

O'Neill's in Allihies

Finally, I had a chance to have a late lunch in O'Neill's Bar and Restaurant in the centre of Allihies. Delicious soup and fresh brown bread went down a treat and I sat outside in the sunshine. O'Neill's is painted a bright red colour and is situated across the road from an equally colourful playground. In fact, the entire village is brightly painted in a variety of colours that make for a wonderful picturesque setting that puts a paint catalogue to shame. I took my time and enjoyed my lunch with my maps, not noticing that I was getting a little sunburned on my head. This made for slightly uncomfortable riding for the rest of the day as my helmet pressed down on my pink pate! Allihies was also well known in the nineteenth century for the nearby copper mines. In 1812, rich deposits of copper were discovered in this area, including one near Ballydonegan, and mined until 1884. At the height of production over 1,500 people were employed by the mines which lead to overcrowding in Allihies where some houses had up to 25 people living in them. The Allihies Copper Mine Museum in the village tells the story of how the Industrial Revolution reached even this remote corner of Ireland.

From Allihies, it is a short ride to another colourful village of Eyeries. It too is painted in all the colours of the rainbow and is decorated with floral displays on many window sills. In 2012 Eyeries won the overall award for the Best Kept Towns in Ireland competition. It is indeed a beautiful well-kept village; slow down and enjoy it as you pass through.

By now I was riding along the Kenmare River near the Cork-Kerry boundary, and shortly after the village of Ardgroom I crossed into County Kerry. I had spent nearly two full fantastic days in Cork and had travelled just over 300 kilometres along its breathtaking coastline.

Ring of Kerry with Skelligs Island

The coast line was broken up the whole way around ever since I left Kinsale. I had seen numerous bays and inlets, cliffs, broken rocks, rugged head lands and wild sandy beaches. My appetite for scenery, historic sites, points of interest that I had never been to before, and wonderful views was getting bigger, so I continued on the Wild Atlantic Way on to the Kingdom of Kerry in search of even more of the wonders that dot our coastline.

Leaving the Old Head of Kinsale
(photo by Kathleen Kelleher)

2

KERRY – THE KINGDOM

I crossed into Kerry late on Saturday afternoon to begin my journey around the coast of the second county on the Wild Atlantic Way. The name 'Kerry' has an interesting origin. It is derived from the son of Fergus, a first century king of Ulster, called Ciar who settled in what is now Kerry. His descendants were called Ciarraighe (pronounced 'Kee ree') and the county eventually was named in Irish as Ciarraí, now anglicised to 'Kerry'. It is also thought that the nickname for the county, 'The Kingdom', may also have originated from 'Ciar's Kingdom'. Kerry of course is also known as one of the wettest places in Ireland, something I would get proof of over the next few days. The Irish record for one-day rainfall is a monsoon-like 243.5 millimetres, recorded in Kerry in September 1993. But riding along by the coast late one sunny afternoon rain was the last thing on my mind.

I had just a little bit of the Beara Peninsula to complete on the way to Kenmare, so once again I took the coast road with the Kenmare River to my left, and the wonderful rock formations of the Caha Mountains to my right. The road is narrow in parts, but this is more than compensated for by the breathtaking views across to the Ring of Kerry, such as at Killmakilloge near the village of Lauragh. My route is tree-lined in several places and goes inland for quite a while. When it reaches the coast again, the trees and high bushes block the view for

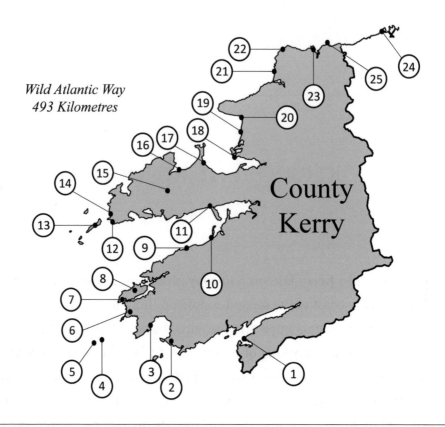

Wild Atlantic Way
493 Kilometres

County
Kerry

Wild Atlantic Way – Kerry Discovery Points

1. *Kilmakilloge Viewpoint*
2. *Coomakesta Pass*
3. *Ballinskelligs Bay*

4. *Little Skellig*
5. *Great Skellig*
6. *Skelligs Viewpoint*

7. *Skellig Rock View*
8. *Geokaun Viewpoint*
9. *Mountain Stage*

10. *Rossbeigh Beach*
11. *Inch Beach*
12. *Slea Head*

13. *Great Blasket Island*
14. *Blasket Sound*
15. *Conor Pass*

16. *Kilcummin Strand*
17. *Castlegregory Beach*
18. *Fenit Beach*

19. *Banna Strand*
20. *Ballyheige Beach*
21. *Ballybunion Beach*

22. *Beal Strand*
23. *Carrigafoyle Castle*
24. *Foynes*

25. *Killimer–Tarbert Ferry*

several kilometres, and it is only closer to Kenmare that it opens up to both the sea and the beautiful Macgillycuddy's Reeks mountain range in the distance.

I reached Kenmare at about 5.00 p.m. and crossed over the river, from which the town gets its name, on Our Lady's Bridge. This iconic bridge with two arches replaced one of Ireland's first suspension bridges in the same location. Unfortunately, this was demolished in 1932 and replaced by the more modern, though dull, concrete structure that exists today. The town of Kenmare dates from the mid-seventeenth century when Oliver Cromwell granted the lands here to the English scientist and philosopher Sir William Petty in payment for mapping Ireland. Sir William is better known as having introduced the concept of *laissez-faire,* warning about over-interference by government in the economy. Today Kenmare is a popular tourist location as it is so close to the trio of tourist attractions: the Beara Peninsula, the Ring of Kerry and the Lakes of Killarney. One unusual fact about the Kenmare locality is that it was home to one Big Bertha, who was a cow that held two Guinness World Records. The first was for breeding a record 39 calves, while the second was for being the oldest cow ever recorded at 49 years and 9 months when she died in 1993. Kenmare marks the start of the 179 kilometre-long Ring of Kerry, and is also known by its Irish name of *An Neidín,* the little nest. Needless to say, an *ohrwurm* of Irish tenor Tommy Fleming singing 'As I Leave Behind Neidín...' invaded my skull and stayed there as I rode away.

Just after leaving Kenmare light rain started and it was time to put on my wet gear for the first time on this journey. Visibility was quite low in places and I could not see much scenery. Despite this, there are some picturesque sections of this coastal road. I particularly enjoyed the tree-lined route to the sharp bend over a small river at Blackwater Bridge, about half way between Kenmare and Sneem. Despite starting to feel a bit wet – water was slowly seeping into my clothes and boots from everywhere – I was aware that it was just as wet for everybody else. I admired the hikers and cyclists who were not letting the rain get the better of them. In Sneem, there were dozens of tourists walking around in shorts and wind-cheaters – perhaps they were optimistic that the weather would get better. So we were all in it together.

Just like in Ballydehob in County Cork, which had its own world wrestling champion, Sneem was home to Steve 'Crusher' Casey, who won a wrestling world title in February 1938. Later that year in September he and Ballydehob's Danno O'Mahony drew their wrestling match in Dublin, and just a month later the two men met again when the 'Crusher' won after 18 rounds and 97 minutes of wrestling. Crusher won several more world titles and the locals in Sneem marked his achievements by erecting a statue to him in the town. They must breed strong men in this part of the world as Sneem is also home to the National Wife Carrying Championships. This is held in July each year as part of the five-day Sneem Family Festival.

After Sneem the road is set back quite a bit from the sea and I travelled inland for several kilometres. I stopped in Castlecove at the 'Wall of Champions' in tribute to local sporting heroes of whom the village is very proud. The champions listed include Joseph White, who was National Cycling Champion from 1952 to 1954; Damien Foxall, winner of the Barcelona World Race for sailing in 2008; and Éamonn Fitzgerald (Eamon Mac Gearailt) who is one of the many unlucky Irish competitors to have finished just outside the medals in the Olympic Games. Fitzgerald finished fourth in the triple jump in the 1932 Games in Los Angeles. A short distance past Castlecove is the Coomakesta Pass where on a fine day there is a grand view overlooking Ballinskelligs Bay.

Arriving in Waterville, the rain started to get heavy and it was time to stop riding. I checked in to the Lodge Hotel where the very helpful owners set me up in my room and insisted on taking my wet gear and drying it in the kitchen. Once refreshed I set out down the main street to the Lobster Bar, which has free WiFi. I checked my email and also

The 'Wall of Champions' in Castlecove

the weather forecast. It was clear from the rain clouds over Kerry on the Met Éireann website that I had made the right decision to stop for the day. I had a deliciously warming hot whiskey after which I felt a lot better. I am dry. I am warm. I am content.

In the early evening the rain at last stopped and I was able to go out and explore Waterville on foot. The village is surrounded by spectacular scenery overlooking Ballinskelligs Bay, and has a wonderful promenade along the beach. The small park beside the beach has statues commemorating two very different famous people: Hollywood's Charlie Chaplin and one of Kerry's best-known sportsmen, Mick O'Dwyer. Micko's statue was unveiled in 2012 and it is dedicated to his sporting achievements in Gaelic football, including his stint as manager of my native Wicklow's county senior football team from 2007 to 2011. Micko certainly had the golden touch, having guided Kerry to eight All-Ireland titles, though even his magic touch did not lead to success for

Wicklow. He is a native of Waterville, and has a pub and guesthouse in the village; he is certainly Watervilles's most famous son.

Charlie Chaplin, on the other hand, used to come here on holidays with his family as he loved the tranquillity and the respect for his privacy that he got from the locals. The annual Charlie Chaplin Comedy Film Festival was set up by local people in his honour, and is now held each August in Waterville where filmmakers compete for the Charlie Award. Both statues to Micko and Charlie are located in a garden dedicated to the memory of a certain T. C. Millerick, who was the village doctor for 11 years. There is a small Celtic cross erected in the garden as a 'token of gratitude' in his honour. Close by there is a Millennium Time Capsule buried under a stone on 10 July 1999, and which will be 'resurrected' on 10 July 2020. I wondered what was in it, but I guess

Charlie Chaplin statue in Waterville

Waterville waterfront in the mist

I'll have to wait until 2020 to find out. Another Celtic cross further up the street commemorates James Butler who owned over 1,400 acres in County Kerry in the 1870s. The Butler family were landlords in this area and their name is also given to the popular Butler Arms Hotel, located behind the cross, which in the past has hosted distinguished guests such as Walt Disney, John Steinbeck and Virginia Woolf, as well as Charlie Chaplin.

For dinner I had delicious fish and chips back at the Lodge Hotel where I realised that I was the only guest staying for the night. It was an eerie feeling to be eating alone in a hotel in the middle of summer. The hotel chef told me that the combination of bad weather and economic recession were having a devastating effect on tourism, and that it would be a long hard summer for the hotel trade. I finished off the evening with a walk along the waterfront and ended up in Mick O'Dwyer's pub where I had a nice pint and a good look at all the photos and news items of the man himself on the pub walls.

View towards Ballinskelligs from Waterville

Leaving Waterville I rode around Ballinskelligs Bay to the village of the same name where I noticed a tower on a piece of land sticking out into the bay. This turned out to be McCarthy's Castle, which is a sixteenth century tower house that belonged to the McCarthy clan, who were chieftains in Kerry and Cork at that time. It was built to protect the bay from pirates, is still in relatively good condition, and is easily accessible from the road. A little further along the road is a small harbour. From here you can see the nearby Horse Island and the ruins of Ballinskelligs Abbey, which was founded as a priory by the Arroasian Canons (named after the diocese of Arras in France) of the Order of St. Augustine in the year 1210. Beside the harbour there are the ruins of another of the many coast guard stations around our coast. Ballinskelligs is a lovely, peaceful place and I feel as if I am the farthest it is possible for me to be from the hustle and bustle of the east coast where I had been only a few days earlier; it is a genuine get-away-from-it-all location. Ballinskelligs of course is closely associated with the Great and Little

Skellig Rocks, which are located just off the end of the peninsula. Great Skellig, also known as Skellig Michael, is listed as a UNESCO World Heritage Site and has a well preserved Christian monastery dating from about the sixth century. There are some excellent views of the Skellig Rocks from St Finian's Bay, where some hardy souls were out surfing. On the way to Valentia Island I stopped in the village of Portmagee at a monument to the many lives lost at sea. Sadly, there is a lot more room for more names to be added. I crossed over to the island where there is the brilliant Skellig Experience Centre beside the bridge, where you can find out all about the Skellig Rocks.

Valentia Island was once an important location in Europe as it is one of the closest places to North America, which is just over 3,000 kilometres to the west. In 1858, a cable connecting Valentia Island to

McCarthy's Castle in Ballinskelligs

St Finian's Bay and Skelligs Rocks

Newfoundland in Canada was laid and became the first communications link across the Atlantic Ocean. The first message was sent on 16 August 1858 from Queen Victoria to US President James Buchanan, which read, 'Glory to God in the highest; on earth, peace and good will toward men'. At the time, the cable was capable of transmitting eight words a minute. However, it was not until the 1860s that the cable operated successfully. A Valentia slate memorial at the side of the road at Foilhummerum Bay marks the site of the 'earliest message sent from Valentia to America'. Valentia slate is also used in the Houses of Parliament in London and the Opera House in Paris. The ruins of the Cable Office, which closed in 1966, are still visible in a field near the memorial. At one time up to 200 people worked there. In many ways, it is sad to think that the iPhone in my pocket is capable of doing more in a few seconds than the Valentia Cable Office could do in a year. In its day it was one of the most amazing technological achievements and

Two views of St Finian's Bay

played a huge role in making the world a smaller place over a hundred years before the creation of the Internet. A short ride away in the main village on the island, Knightstown, the Heritage Museum has a great display of photos and artefacts about the cable which put Valentia on the world map.

Riding across Valentia Island there are fantastic views of the Portmagee Channel and Valentia Harbour from the high narrow roads such as at Geokaun View. In Knightstown there is a short ferry to Reenard near Cahirciveen on the mainland. While waiting for the ferry I checked out the Town Clock in the harbour which was built in the late nineteenth century. There was also a scales on this spot where coal was weighed by the Valentia Slab Company, which worked the slate mentioned earlier. According to a plaque on the clock tower, 'the process of weighing the coal was interesting – when horse and cart was the mode of transport, the cart was first weighed, the coal was then loaded and the difference was what was paid for'.

Portmagee Channel at Valentia Island

Ballycarbery Castle

Arriving in Cahirciveen there was heavy traffic due to a road accident. While waiting for a chance to get through I noticed signs for a barracks and for Ballycarbery Castle, so I decided to take a look. The barracks is on the edge of the town and was once the location for the local Royal Irish Constabulary (RIC). It was built in the late nineteenth century and has been restored making for an imposing building with a fairytale-style tower. It is now a heritage centre and features exhibits on Daniel O'Connell, the Fenian uprising of 1867, and the 1916 Easter rebellion. I continued on for about three kilometres towards Doulus Head to see the large ruins of Ballycarbery Castle. This castle was reputedly built in the sixteenth century and was later captured by Oliver Cromwell's parliamentarian forces who caused a lot of damage to it. The ruins are partially covered with ivy, but once again I stand in awe at what must have been a fantastic castle in its day, wondering what our sixteenth century ancestors thought of it all.

Back in Cahirciveen I stopped on the edge of the town at a small garden memorial park which marks the birthplace of Daniel O'Connell, known as the 'Liberator'. I looked around the garden and wondered at how such a colossus of early nineteenth century politics in Ireland could have had such humble beginnings. A sign at the garden tells us that the town of Cahirciveen was founded by O'Connell in 1801, and that a local church was dedicated to his name. A famous, though distant, relative of mine is buried in the graveyard of this church. My dad had often mentioned that our family was related to Monsignor Hugh O'Flaherty, who was best known as the 'Vatican Pimpernel' for saving over 6,000 downed pilots, Jews and escaped allied prisoners in Rome during World War II. I have worked out in my family tree that he is my third cousin once removed, and I am related to him through my paternal grandfather's family. He died in 1963 when I was just four years

Outside Cahirciveen

Main Street, Killorglin

old, but of course I did not know him. The 1983 film *The Scarlet and the Black*, starring Gregory Peck as Monsignor O'Flaherty, is based on his exploits in the Vatican in defying the occupying Germans. He was a true hero of World War II.

Riding towards Killorglin, I stopped briefly for views out over Dingle Bay towards the mountains on the Dingle Peninsula at Mountain Stage, and the beautiful Rossbeigh Beach near the village of Glenbeigh. In the centre of Killorglin I stopped for petrol where I met a Swiss biker, Leila, who was also filling up. We got chatting and it turned out she was touring the Ring of Kerry as well. We went for a coffee and a chat to compare notes at the Zest Café. We had parked right in the centre of Killorglin which is famous for the annual Puck Fair held each August. For a short time I was a tour guide explaining to her that the central character in Puck Fair is a goat who is made 'King Puck' for the duration of the fair. Oliver Cromwell may have been the person responsible for the legend of King Puck. While pillaging the surrounding countryside, Cromwell's soldiers reputedly scattered a herd of goats, one of which made it to Killorglin. The exhausted male (puck) goat's arrival allegedly alerted the townspeople of impending danger and they were able to prepare to defend themselves. Today we can see some preparations being made for the Puck Fair, especially for King Puck who will spend a lot of time in a cage elevated over the town square during the fair.

Killorglin marks the end of the Ring of Kerry for me. While it continues on towards Killarney, I decide to ride northwards towards the village of Castlemaine on the road to Tralee. The well-known traditional Irish-Australian song, 'The Wild Colonial Boy', is based on Jack Duggan who was 'born and reared in Ireland, in a place called Castlemaine'. A pub bearing his name is at the centre of the village. He seems to have been a bit of a Robin Hood character as the song claims that 'he robbed the rich, he helped the poor', but he met his end in 1830 according to the song when 'a bullet pierced his proud young heart'. Castlemaine takes its name from a castle built here in the sixteenth century. It was destroyed by none other than Oliver Cromwell's troops, who were probably running away from King Puck in Killorglin at the time. It was now late afternoon and instead of turning left towards the Dingle Peninsula I headed off in the direction of Tralee to spend the night at the Ballingarry House hotel where my wife Roma had come down from Dublin by train for the weekend. Roma would join me for a day on my Wild Atlantic Way tour.

It was a quiet Sunday morning when we set out and headed west along the northern side of the Dingle peninsula in an anti-clockwise direction around the coast. The Wild Atlantic Way criss-crosses the Dingle Peninsula so it doesn't really matter which way you go. We first checked out the Blennerville Windmill on the outskirts of Tralee, where you can see the workings of the largest and oldest working windmill in Ireland. Originally built in 1800, it fell into ruin around 1850 but was eventually restored in 1990. Blennerville was also the main port of emigration from Kerry to America during the Great Famine. For several years, starting in 1848, the famine ship *Jeannie Johnston* carried over

Blennerville Windmill in Tralee

2,500 emigrants in cramped conditions on the seven-week journey across the Atlantic. Amazingly, not one life was lost on the ship in that time. I have been on board the replica of this ship, which is tied up on the River Liffey in Dublin only a few metres from my place of work, and can testify to the cramped conditions.

By way of demonstrating to Roma what the Wild Atlantic Way was all about, I turned down a random lane towards the beach at Cappa-clogh where there is a Seaside Caravan and Camping Park. We spotted a metal statue of a man looking out to the sea overlooking the beach.

Maharee Islands with Kerry Head in the distance

A Morris Minor in the fields on the Maharees Peninsula

Cappaclogh is the location of the annual Irish Bog Snorkelling Championships and the All-Ireland Currach Bog Paddlers Race. We continued on to Castlegregory, which is a lovely town with a market that day and a traffic problem to match; it took quite some time to get through even though we were on a bike. Not surprisingly, the village gets its name from somebody called Gregory who lived in a local castle. Gregory Hoare built the castle where the village is now situated in the sixteenth century. This unfortunate Gregory is reported to have dropped dead in the doorway of his castle on the day of his son Hugh's wedding to the daughter of one of his arch enemies. He was trying to prevent his enemy entering his castle – something which would not have been a problem today in the midst of heavy traffic. Castlegregory also marks the start of the Maharees Peninsula, at the end of which are the Maharees Islands, also known as the Seven Hogs. We stopped at the end of

Brandon Bay

The author at Mount Brandon Point

the peninsula at a small harbour and looked out at the uninhabited flat islands which were just visible in the mist. Somewhere in the distance to the north was Kerry Head, and to the west was Mount Brandon, which was our next destination.

Leaving the Maharees we travelled back through Castlegregory, which by now was almost completely blocked with traffic and took ages to get through. The road to Mount Brandon is flanked by Stradbally Mountain to the left, and Brandon Bay to the right. While we could see out to sea quite a lot, the tops of the mountains were covered in mist. The beach at Kilcummin, at 19 kilometres, is the longest in Ireland. At the end of this road, which is a cul-de-sac, is Brandon Point. However Mount Brandon, which at 952 metres is the ninth highest mountain in Ireland, was nowhere to be seen due to mist. We posed for some photos and even climbed up part of the nearby hill to try to get a better look at the mountain, but to no avail. Mount Brandon is named after St Brendan the Navigator, who is also the patron saint of Kerry. Legend has it that he climbed to the top of the mountain to see America before he set out on his epic voyage across the Atlantic. Because of its association with St Brendan, the mountain is also a place of pilgrimage to a cross at the peak. On our way back down the same road we stopped in the small vil-

O'Donnell's Bar in An Clochán

lage of An Clochán, which is part of the Kerry Gaeltacht, at O'Donnell's Pub for a *cupán tae*. As we were in the Gaeltacht we tried to be *ag caint Gaeilge* as best we could. By now it was about midday and we were the

Inside O'Donnell's Bar

View towards Dingle Harbour

only people in the pub. There is something about going into a pub with no one else there – it is almost an invasion of privacy. Nevertheless, we had a very nice cuppa and we viewed the fantastic collection of beer mats on the beams across the ceiling. With lots of other old tools and instruments hanging on the wall, O'Donnell's is certainly a great place to stop on this road.

As there is no coast road around the northern side of Mount Brandon, it is necessary to travel inland in order to get to the other side of the mountain. This road goes through the Conor Pass which involves a steep ride up and down both sides of the pass. I had to be a bit more careful on the bike as it handles differently with two people on it. Buses and trucks are not allowed on this road and it is easy to see why. The road is so narrow in places that even on a bike I often had to pull in to let oncoming cars pass by. However, the sharp bends and narrow passages were the least of my worries. Not long after the start of the climb we were surrounded by a thick mist, with visibility down to less than five metres in places. Luckily, we had a careful driver in front of us and we followed his bright red fog lights all the way up to the top of the pass, where we thanked him for showing us the way. The pass is only five kilometres long, but it feels much longer due to the slow pace. This was definitely one of the twistiest but most exciting rides I have ever had.

We stopped at the top of the pass and through gaps in the mist we had a taste of the wonderful viewpoint that gives the Conor Pass its deserved reputation as a must-see location on the Dingle Peninsula. Coming down was a bit easier and it seemed like it was no time before we descended out of the mist to a breathtaking view over the town of Dingle. As Dingle is the only way in and out of the rest of the Dingle Peninsula, we decided we would continue our tour and stop there on the way back. We arrived back at the coast in Murreagh where we stopped at the ruins of the twelfth century Hiberno-Romanesque Kilmalkedar Church. This historic site is associated with St Brendan

St. Brendan's House beside Kilmalkedar Church

and has interesting Ogham stones, and a standing stone sundial. Murreagh is also home to one of the Dingle Peninsula's most well-known archaeological sites, the Gallarus Oratory. This early Christian church is over 1,000 years old with walls made of sandstone that are over one metre wide. Though quite small it's very dry inside. This unmissable gem of a boat-shaped building is a tribute to those who built it so long ago in that it is still standing today. I and many other tourists there today gaze in wonder at this simple but wonderful building. Nearby is the less spectacular Gallarus Castle which dates from the fifteenth century.

We passed through Ballyferriter and took the short ride up to Smerwick to see *Dún an Óir*, Fort of Gold, which was the site of a terrible massacre of over 400 Italian and Spanish Papal troops in 1580. This location is also called *Fort del Oro* in Spanish. The troops had been sent to help the Irish during the Desmond Rebellion against Elizabeth I, but were quickly trapped at Smerwick. Hopelessly outnumbered, they

Gallarus Oratory

surrendered to the English who promptly ordered that all except officers be beheaded and their bodies thrown into the sea. Another name for this site is the 'Field of the Heads', as the victims' heads are presumed to have been buried there. Two Englishmen reputedly present at the massacre were Sir Walter Raleigh, then a captain, and the poet Edmund Spenser. The site is accessible through a narrow lane at the end of which is a poignant stone monument featuring a cross on one side and 'floating' heads on the other. It is a truly awful thing to contemplate that these men and women from Spain and Italy who came to help the Irish in their rebellion were massacred on the spot where they landed. This dreadful day in Irish history is also a black mark on English history as well.

We arrived at Dunquin at the end of the peninsula, where we saw the Blasket Islands, which to people of my generation were considered the most bleak and miserable place in Ireland to have lived. This impression comes from the book *Peig* by Peig Sayers, who lived on the islands. This book was required reading for generations of students learning Irish in secondary school. Life on the Blaskets was tough as the land was very poor and the inhabitants depended on fishing for a living. The population of the island declined so much that it was abandoned in 1953 when all the inhabitants, including Peig herself, moved to the mainland.

Dunquin is the most westerly settlement in Ireland, and the nearby Gauraun Point is the most westerly point of mainland Ireland. Some people refer to this location as the 'next parish to America'. Just past the village is the Blasket Island Centre where we went to escape a shower. The Centre describes the real hardships of a life of subsistence on the islands. It also features exhibitions on the traditional way of life of the islanders and the extraordinary amount of literature produced by the island's inhabitants. This is definitely a place to visit by anyone touring the Dingle peninsula. When we finally got to Slea Head the famous views towards the Ring of Kerry to the south were partially blotted out by the Kerry mist. We decided to move on and find a place where we could sit down and enjoy a leisurely lunch, which we did in The Skipper Restaurant in Ventry. I had French seafood soup while Roma had prawns which arrived at our table on fire! Delicious, and just the thing to warm us up on a misty day.

Back in Dingle after lunch we stopped for a quick walkabout and then made straight for the most famous pub in Dingle – Dick Mack's. There was traditional Irish music playing in the packed bar where there is a fantastic array of bottles of all types of drinks behind the counter. Outside we checked the Hollywood Walk of Fame-style pavement to see names like Robert Mitchum, Tom Cruise, Julia Roberts and Dolly Parton embedded on the ground. Dingle is a well-known tourist destination, and on a damp Sunday afternoon all the pubs were full of them. In addition to famous movie stars and tourists, Dingle was said to have almost become a safe haven for one of the eighteenth century's most famous and tragic women, Marie Antoinette, Queen of France. In 1789, three Kerrymen, including James Rice of Dingle, attempted to rescue her from prison in Paris during the Revolution. They had bribed the gaolers and had teams of horses ready to take her to the coast where a wine ship was waiting to take her to Dingle. At the eleventh hour she refused to abandon her husband, King Louis XVI, and remained in Paris where of course she met her end at the guillotine in 1793. Quite what she would have made of Dingle would have been an interesting topic for discussion over a few pints in Dick Mack's. Perhaps she might have said to the Irish, 'Let them eat spuds!'

By now we were on the way back along the southern side of the peninsula to Tralee, and we made just two more stops. The first was at the South Pole Inn in Annascaul, where a hero of mine, Antarctic explorer Tom Crean, used to live. I had read Michael Smith's excellent biography of Crean, *An Unsung Hero,* where he described Crean as 'one of the greatest characters in the history of polar exploration'. Anyone who has read this book or any other account of Sir Ernest Shackleton's

South Pole Inn in Annascaul

unsuccessful expedition to cross the Antarctic in 1914 cannot fail to admire the exploits of Shackleton, Crean and their comrades. Crean was one of six men, including Shackleton, who sailed on an epic voyage of 1,200 kilometres in a small boat across the South Atlantic to the island of South Georgia in 1916. In 1927, he opened the South Pole Inn whose walls are adorned with photographs of his expeditions. I feel almost in awe of him as I sit in his pub and drink a glass of 'Creans' beer, which is brewed in Dingle. He lived in Annascaul until 1938 when this tough explorer was felled by a burst appendix. Across the road from the pub is a small garden with a life-sized statue of Crean holding two puppies; he had a life-long passion for animals. Our second stop was to look out over Inch Beach, which despite its name is almost five kilometres long. This was a location for the 1970 movie *Ryan's Daughter*, which was directed by David Lean and starred Gregory Peck. This movie is credited with putting the Dingle Peninsula on the tourist map with its portrayal of majestic landscapes and panoramic views.

By now it was early evening and it was time to head back to Tralee for a well-earned dinner. We had a great day despite some rain, and it was hugely enjoyable to have Roma with me for the day. The Dingle Peninsula is a wonderful bike ride of 225 kilometres with excellent roads which took the full day to complete. We spent the evening in Tralee and had dinner at the excellent Cassidy's restaurant in Abbey Street. Tralee was full of life in the evening and I'm sure it would be a great location for a holiday so it was a pity our time there was so short. The Ballingarry House hotel where we were staying, previously called The Manhattan Hotel, was built in the eighteenth century and still retains its classic Georgian charms. Just down the road is a super bronze sculpture of four Kerry footballers leaping high to catch a ball. They take their Gaelic football very seriously in the Kingdom, and with hundreds of All-Ireland medals in Kerrymen's pockets, it is no wonder that they are passionate about their sport. The sculpture is in the middle of a roundabout, so it is not that easy to see up close.

Next morning after breakfast I dropped Roma off to the train station for the late morning train to Dublin. My target today was to reach County Clare, with the ferry across the Shannon Estuary at Tarbert being my last location in the Kingdom. But first, a tour of the North Kerry coast awaited and I rode out of Tralee to Fenit. The name Fenit is based on the Irish name *An Fhianait,* which means 'Wild Place', though today it was nice and calm. At the end of the pier here is the St Brendan the Navigator Heritage Park. I chatted to man named Derek who pointed out the Little Samphire Island Lighthouse, and Mount Brandon on the Dingle Peninsula which I could not see yesterday. He also told me that several German bombers crashed into the mountain during World War II, and that there was always a rush by him and other local boys to get bits of the aircraft as souvenirs after each crash. St Brendan the Navigator, whose statue looks out to sea, was born in the year 484 near

St Brendan the Navigator Heritage Park

Little Samphire Island Lighthouse

At Fenit Pier looking over Dingle Bay

here on Fenit Island. A small stone memorial beside the beach marks the place of his birth, but be warned: it is easy to miss. Fenit is actually divided into two parts according to my map, Fenit Within and Fenit Without. These names refer to the walled protection that once surrounded parts of the island to dissuade invaders from the mainland, which is connected to the island by a long sandbar that is not accessible today by a Harley-Davidson motorcycle.

I made my way from Fenit to Ardfert to see the magnificent ruins of its cathedral, which was once the ecclesiastical capital of Kerry. St Brendan the Navigator founded a monastery here in the sixth century, but the current ruins date from the twelfth century. Unfortunately, it was burned down in 1641 and has stood as a ruin since. I toured the inside of the cathedral which has some very informative and interesting exhibitions. But the crowning glory is the ruin itself. These walls have stood for about 900 years, though today they are supported by steel poles that were recently added to the walls, which appear to be bulging somewhat. I was told this by the very helpful OPW staff who also told me that there had been many burials under the floor of the cathedral as was the fashion in many others. The OPW guide informed me that only wealthy people could afford to do this, and that most of the graves were shallow which lead to a bad smell during religious ceremonies.

Inside Ardfert Cathedral

Hence the expression 'stinking rich'. After my tour I stopped at the slightly quirky Glandore Gate nearby, where there is a bookshop and tearoom where I had tea and apple tart with Ron the chatty owner. This tearoom has a very interesting collection of second hand books and is worth stopping for a browse.

Not long after leaving Ardfert I noticed a road signposted for Banna Strand, which was once voted in the top ten 'Go To Breathtaking Beaches' in the world by TripAdvisor. Most students of Irish history will also know it as the location where the Irish patriot Sir Roger Casement landed from a German submarine on 21 April 1916 to take part in the Easter Rising. He was quickly captured, brought to the Tower of London, and later hanged for treason, the last of the 1916 leaders to be executed. The simple, but rather bleak, monument to him and his companion Robert Monteith, who escaped capture, commemorates

Ballyheige Castle in the mist

Casement for 'furthering the cause of Irish freedom'. A much more fitting memorial to Casement is the very fine statue of him in the nearby village of Ballyheige, where he is depicted wearing handcuffs in a small garden at the beginning of the long Ballyheige beach. Across the road from the garden is the magnificent gate into Ballyheige Golf Club where you can also see the impressive ruins of Ballyheige Castle, which was built in 1810 but burned down in 1840 and again in 1921. A plaque on the wall at the gate commemorates the eighteenth century economist Richard Cantillon who was born in Ballyheige. He is described as the 'Fa-

Roger Casement statue in Ballyheige

ther of Modern Economics' and the first theorist to define the role of an 'entrepreneur'. After Ballyheige the Wild Atlantic Way circles around the narrow lanes of Kerry Head. It is from here you will get your first glimpse of Loop Head in County Clare in the distance to the north. At the centre of the circle are the Triskmore and Maulin mountains, but they look more like flat hills in this rather featureless landscape.

I continued northwards through the quiet villages of Causeway and Ballyduff, between which there is the well preserved Rattoo Round Tower down a lane off the main road. The tower dates from the early twelfth century and stands about 27 metres high, and on this day was surrounded with scaffolding for restoration work. There is no access to the inside of the tower where there is one of the best examples of a *Sheela na gig* in Britain and Ireland carved on the north

*Rattoo Round Tower
undergoing repairs*

window facing inwards. These explicit carvings of a woman were said to keep evil spirits away, and at Rattoo it is the only example of one in an Irish round tower. Beside the tower are the ruins of a church which is used as a cemetery with a variety of vaults that look like small houses. At the north end of the village of Ballyduff is a crossroads. To the right is the road to Ballybunnion, to the left is the Coast Road, but straight ahead is a small road to the Rattoo Heritage Museum and Interpretative Centre which overlooks the River Feale. This was not sign-posted

Taking the Coast Road in Ballyduff

so it is easy to miss, but worth checking out to find out more about this fascinating area.

Ballybunnion is North Kerry's most famous seaside resort and as I rode towards this legendary holiday destination it is not hard to see why. On the approach to Ballybunnion the world famous golf links of the same name is on the left side between the road and the sea. There were plenty of golfers out enjoying their round of golf, and as I rode by unprotected on my motorcycle I hoped there would be no wayward shots on to the road. One of the most famous visitors to this golf club was the former President of the United States, Bill Clinton. In 2009

Ballybunnion Castle

Statue of President Bill Clinton in Ballybunnion

he named the course here as his favourite place to play, and there is a statue honouring him outside the Garda station on the Main Street. Ballybunnion has not one, but two magnificent golden sandy beaches surrounded by cliffs. I decided to park the bike and take one of the many cliff walks available down to the ruins of Ballybunnion Castle which overlook both beaches. The castle was built in the fourteenth century, but was destroyed in 1582 during the Desmond Rebellions. Only the east wall now remains, but it still stands out in pride of place between the two beaches. These cliffs were a taster for what is to come on the rest of the North Kerry coast and on into County Clare. Just past Ballybunnion are the Bromore Cliffs where you will find interesting names for the features here, such as The Mermaid's Caves, The Devil's Castle, and The Last Steps.

I continued on northwards until I reached the River Shannon Estuary at Beal Strand, which is a rocky beach covered in green algae when I stopped there. The estuary is the largest in Ireland and was busy with shipping, no doubt sailing up to the Alumina Plant at Aughinish or to deliver fuel to Shannon Airport. My next stop was at the wonderful Carrigafoyle Castle near Ballylongford. While the castle is now a ruin, it still looks almost intact and has a considerable amount of the walls built in the 1490s still standing. The castle is tower-shaped, and at five stories is over 26 metres high, and it is possible to climb up the 104 steps of the spiral staircase inside all the way to the top. Along the way there are several floors where you can see what the building might have been like to live in at the end of the Middle Ages, including what looks like a double toilet with a wooden seat. The castle was once known as the Guardian of the Shannon due to its location, but in 1580, during a siege, the west facing wall was knocked down with just a few cannon shots crushing to death many of the defenders inside.

Beal Strand at the Shannon Estuary

Carrigafoyle Castle

I finally reached my point of departure from Kerry at the town of Tarbert in the late afternoon. I was just in time to see the Tarbert Bridewell Courthouse and Jail Museum before it closed. The building ceased to be a jail in 1874, but it continued as a courthouse for another 75 years. Here you can see life-size models of judges, police, prison guards and of course some prisoners. Justice in the nineteenth century was tough and you can learn about how it was meted out at the exhibition here.

At Tarbert the Wild Atlantic Way branches to Foynes in County Limerick. The road from Tarbert to Foynes runs right alongside the Shannon Estuary and through the village of Glin. This small village is well-known as the location of Glin Castle, an eighteenth century Georgian building that was formerly the home of the Knight of Glin, and which is now a hotel. During the late 1930s and early 1940s, Foynes was one of the busiest passenger airports in Europe. At that time fly-

Tarbert Bridewell Courthouse and Jail

ing boats were used to transport passengers across the Atlantic, which made Foynes' location on the edge of Europe an ideal place to set up an airport. The advent of a new land-based airport at Shannon in 1942 spelled the end for the Foynes flying boats. However, the Foynes Flying Boat Museum recalls the glory days when famous people such as Bob Hope, Ernest Hemmingway, Merle Oberon and John F. Kennedy stopped in Foynes on their way to and from America. The highlight of the museum is a replica of a Boeing 314 Clipper. You can see the distinctive three-part tail fin sticking out of the plane's protective shed from the main road.

I rode back along the same coast road towards Tarbert to take the ferry to Killimer in County Clare just as it started to rain heavily. At the ferry terminal I met a young Canadian couple from Vancouver who were making a tour of southwest Ireland by bicycle, and they too were getting wet. We shared jokes about rainfall, bragging about who has the wettest climate and whether Ireland or Western Canada gets the most rain. They told me that Vancouver is one of the wettest places in Canada and I felt a little bit better knowing that there was somewhere else in the world where people might be getting wetter than me. Waiting for the ferry I had some time to think back on my few days in Kerry and the 493 kilometres that I had travelled. I had seen some of the most beautiful sights and locations that this part of southwest Ireland has to offer on the Wild Atlantic Way. The Kingdom is a fascinating county and I loved its coastline all the way around the peninsulas and mountains. It's no wonder that tourists have been coming here for hundreds of years. I leave with fond memories to treasure as I cross the Shannon Estuary to County Clare.

Waiting for the ferry in Tarbert

3

CLARE – CLIFFS AND MUCH MORE

I t is early evening as I arrive in the small village of Killimer on the ferry from Tarbert. The rain had stopped and the early evening sun welcomed me to County Clare. This county was once part of the province of Connaught, but became part of Munster in the early seventeenth century. Clare is known as the 'Banner County', and it's thought that this nickname came from the tradition of carrying banners at monster meetings held by Daniel O'Connell during his by-election campaign to become Westminster MP for the constituency of Clare in 1828. I rode the 9 kilometres from Killimer to Kilrush where I decided to stop for the day.

When I arrived in Kilrush I needed to get out of my wet gear. The first place I spotted that had a sign for accommodation was Crotty's pub on Market Square in the centre of the town, so I parked my bike outside and entered the bar to enquire about a room. Crotty's is a popular and very busy pub but I didn't mind waiting. I was given a room upstairs over the bar and I carried up all my gear from the bike to dry out anything that was wet. While doing this, the kind staff of the pub offered a safe place in a yard behind the bar to park my bike. So for the last time today, I got up on the bike and parked it in the yard. The staff helped me with a heater to dry my things, and allowed me to use the nearby sitting room to dry out the rest of my gear. So far on this trip

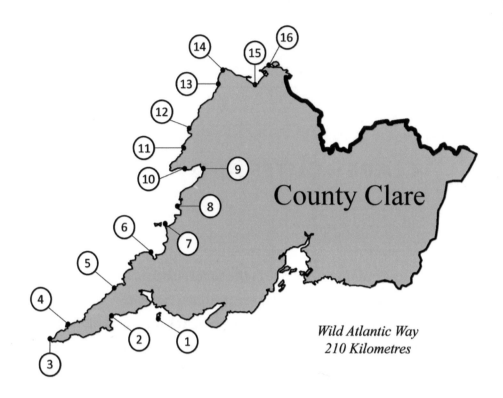

Wild Atlantic Way: Clare Discovery Points

1. Scattery Island

2. Carrigaholt Bay

3. Loop Head

4. Bridges of Ross

5. Kilkee Cliffs

6. White Strand Doonbeg

7. Mutton Island View

8. Spanish Point

9. Lahinch Beach

10. Liscannor Bay View

11. Cliffs of Moher

12. Doolin Port

13. Fanore Beach

14. Black Head

15. Ballyvaughan Pier

16. Flaggy Shore

I have been amazed at the hospitality that I have received everywhere I have been. My stuff was all over the place, but at least everything had started to dry out. Bangers and Mash were on the pub menu and I couldn't think of anything that would make a heartier meal which I washed down with a delicious pint of Guinness. Crotty's is a well-known traditional music pub in Kilrush and there was a great session on in the bar while I was there. On the wall outside the pub you can easily see why this pub is popular with musicians as a plaque commemorates Elizabeth Crotty who established the pub and is described as the 'First Lady of Concertina'. In the 1950s she was one of the best known and highly respected traditional musicians in Ireland.

After dinner I wandered about the town of Kilrush. It was very quiet with almost empty streets this evening. Just across from Crotty's pub in the Market Square is a monument commemorating the Manchester

Crotty's pub, Kilrush

Martyrs: Allen, Larkin and O'Brien. These three Fenians, in one of the last public executions in England, were hanged together for the murder of a policeman in 1867. In a classic example of how one man's terrorist is another man's freedom fighter, in Ireland we call these men martyrs whereas in England the murder of the policeman is known as part of the Manchester Outrages. The monument in Kilrush was built in 1903 and features a statue of the Maid of Erin with an Irish wolfhound at her feet.

Just down the wide street towards the marina is a plaque on a bridge dedicated to Martin Frank McMahon who 'died that others might live' in 1956. I wondered who he was and what sacrifice he had made. It turns out that he had witnessed an accident at this spot where two men on a bicycle with no brakes had crashed into the river, and he drowned in an effort to save one of the men.

Off the coast from the Kilrush Marina is Scattery Island, where there are the ruins of a monastery and a round tower which at over 34 metres is one of the highest in Ireland. A settlement was first founded in the early sixth century on the island by St Senan. One local legend says that he first banished a serpent from the island, but that he banned women as well. Today you can get a ferry from Kilrush to the island where there are many ruins to see.

Next morning I had a monstrous breakfast during which I had an interesting chat about emigration with an *Irish Independent* journalist who was also staying in Crotty's. Apparently many parts of Clare are losing a lot of young people to emigration and that this is being especially felt by GAA clubs. He told me that it is estimated that in one nearby village, more than 100 people under the age of 30 have emigrated in the past three years. I leave Crotty's with fond memories of the hospitality provided to me there.

Just a few kilometres outside Kilrush was my first stop at the West Clare Railway in a place called Moynasta. This is a historical narrow gauge railway which was restored in the 1990s after it was closed in

West Clare Railway at Moynasta

1961. It was first started in 1885, with Charles Stewart Parnell turning the first sod. The famed locomotive, the *Slieve Callan*, and two carriages were parked on the railway line at the side of the road. It was still early morning and it had not yet set out on its tours for the day. Songwriter Percy French parodied the West Clare Railway when he wrote the famous song 'Are Ye Right There, Michael?' in 1897 after he was delayed for a concert in Kilkee because of a slow train and the decision of the driver to stop for no apparent reason. An *ohrwurm* invades my head and I continue my journey with the chorus of French's song for the next few kilometres hoping that I'll 'be there before the night' wherever 'there' will be tonight!

The journey out to the end of Loop Head is through mainly flat land and makes for a nice ride with the sea visible on both sides. I stopped briefly at Carrigaholt where there are lovely views out over the Shannon Estuary towards North Kerry. From a long distance away you can also see the formidable looking Carrigaholt Castle standing guard over the River Shannon. The castle was built in the mid-fifteenth century by the McMahon family who were then chiefs of the Loop Head peninsula. It is a five story tower shape, but it is now in ruin and you cannot enter the building though it is possible to walk around it. Slightly further along the road I stopped at another ruin near a place called Cross. This was a ruined church in the middle of a graveyard. Inside the church the floor was nearly covered in headstones and, like at Ardfert, I wondered if the 'stinking rich' were buried there.

Church ruin and graveyard near Cross

Kilbaha Memorial Park

I was getting closer to Loop Head when I spotted an interesting looking small memorial park near Kilbaha. The park is located across the road from Keating's Bar and commemorates the events here during the Fenian Rising of 1867. The Fenian Rising was a complete failure nationwide, and events here fared no better. Five local rebels tried to take over the local coast guard station, but were not successful. The ruins of the same station are still visible from the road. Two of the men were captured and jailed. The park notices also tell us about the Grave of Yellow Men. Nine men, possibly from China or Japan, lost their lives here in the late 1800s and were buried by the roadside a little bit further back on the road. A new nine stone memorial marks the spot where they were supposedly buried. Also mentioned here is the Kilballyowen Scroll. The scroll is a display of carved metal illustrations depicting local religion, music, farming, fishing, emigration and sport. Finally, the small park has a small monument of a boy and girl at a tree. This little park is a gem and well worth stopping at, though be prepared for a long read of all the notices to figure out what it is all about.

I was now finally on my way to Loop Head. The road is a pleasant ride with flat country on each side of the road. At the end of Loop Head is the lighthouse. I took the tour which brought me to the top of the tower. It is very interesting how the lighthouse works and well worth the €5.00 entry fee. There is a fantastic view up the coast from the balcony. At the top of the lighthouse, I asked another tourist to take a photo with small cliffs in the background. These aren't the Cliffs of Moher, which are further up the coast, but they serve as a spectacular appetizer nonetheless. There has been a lighthouse here since 1670, and some of the original buildings still remain beside the tower which itself was built in 1854. Our guide also told us that the message 'Eire 45' was laid out in whitewashed stone just beneath the lighthouse during the Second World War to warn potential invaders and shipping that they were close to neutral Ireland.

There are also some details on the workings of the lighthouse in the small museum which is part of the complex. It tells us more about the lighthouse during the Second World War. Located here also is one of 83 look-out posts (LOPs) that dotted the coast every 15 kilometres or so. Each LOP was manned by soldiers around the clock from 1939 to 1945. The 'Eire 45' sign was also one of 83 similar signs around our coast (numbered 1–83), which warned pilots that they were flying over Ireland. This was a simple idea to alert the pilots of where they were in the pre-GPS days of navigation. The museum also tells the interesting story of respect for a dead seaman, who was washed up underneath the cliffs at Loop Head in 1940. His head, arms and legs were missing, but despite this local Gardaí recovered his body in a 'daring and risky plan'. They lowered two men down the cliff face by rope to recover the seaman. Despite the many tattoos on his body, he was never identified. Loop Head is one of the best discovery points on the Wild Atlantic Way and one of the most memorable ones I have visited so far. It is definitely worth a visit by anyone touring this area.

Loop Head Lighthouse

I ride back along the road I came from and turned off after just a few kilometres to see the Bridges of Ross cliff formations. There is only one 'bridge' still standing and it is just a short walk from the car park to see the rock arch that gives this place its name. The rock formations here are a popular place for rare birds to nest and is a well-known destination for bird watchers. All along the coast here are spectacular rock formations in many places such as at Kilkee Cliffs. The land here is still relatively flat and I can see the coast to my left almost continuously on this west Clare route. In the seaside resort of Kilkee I rode along the Strand Line which runs around the horseshoe-shaped bay where today there were people sitting on the steps at the northern end taking in the sun. This is a beautiful road with many of the cottages that line the route featuring large bay windows looking out over the bay. At the extreme southern end of this road is a life-size statue of the Limerick-born actor Richard Harris. This statue was unveiled by another famous actor, Russell Crowe, in 2006. It shows him as a young man playing tennis facing out to sea. He had a deep affection for Kilkee, even naming his house in the Bahamas after the town. I rode down to the south-

Kilkee

Mosaic by artist Carl Moynihan

ern end of the bay hoping to continue on along the coast line, but the roads ends in a cul-de-sac at the Kilkee golf club.

At Doonbeg I turn off to check out the White Strand at the end of a long lane. Here there is a memorial to one of Ireland's greatest athletes, Pat "Babe" McDonald, who was born in Doonbeg. Competing for the United States of America he won gold medals at the 1912 Olympic Games in Stockholm for the shot put, and at the 1920 Games in Antwerp for the 56-pound weight throw.

In Quilty I stopped to admire a mosaic, created by artist Carl Moynihan, on a small wall at the start of the bay on which the village is located. It depicts the rescue of sailors from a French ship, the *Leon XIII*, which was making its way to America when it crashed on to the rocks during a severe storm in 1907. The mosaic shows us that local fishermen used currachs to rescue the crew. One of the crew was later quoted as saying, 'I have been all over the world, but never, never, in my life have I seen any action more heroic than the conduct of the Clare fishermen'. The local church, which features a distinctive, early Christian-like round tower, was built in remembrance of the rescue. The bell from the ship is on display in the church. You can also see Mutton Island from here. St Senan, mentioned earlier, is reputed to have founded a church on the island in the sixth century. In more recent times the island was used as a detention camp during the independence struggle in the early 1920s.

Milltown Malbay is the self-styled home of traditional Irish music. There are live music sessions on somewhere in the town seven days a week. The well-known Willie Clancy Summer School is held here every July when students from every part of the world learn about Irish music, song and dance. It is only late morning as I pass through the busy streets of Milltown Malbay, so I'll have to wait for another day to sample the Irish music there. Very close to Milltown Malbay is the small village of Spanish Point. It gets its name from the unfortunate Spanish ships and sailors who were part of the Spanish Armada in 1588 that were shipwrecked near here during stormy weather. Many of these sailors are reputed to have been buried on Mutton Island.

About halfway between Milltown Malbay and Lahinch, I stopped at the side of the road to take a look at a monument to 'Rineen'. It is located on a dangerous bend, and it commemorates the 'gallant stand made at this spot against the forces of British oppression on the 22nd day of Sept, 1920'. This is also known as the Rineen Ambush in which the IRA killed six policemen. In savage reprisals, British forces killed five local people and burnt some houses and shops in the surrounding area. Thankfully, it is a lot more peaceful today, and as I was getting back onto the bike I was hailed by the two Canadians on their bicycles whom I had met yesterday on the ferry at Tarbert. Like me they had dried out, had cheered up, and were heading for the Cliffs.

At Lahinch (also spelled 'Lehinch') I avoided the main streets and instead rode around by the beach on the coastal route around the town. This is a holiday resort and there are a lot of shiny new houses and mobile home parks facing out to sea. The road out of Lahinch passes between two golf clubs, The Castle and Lahinch. There are lots of golfers out this morning, and while I am envious of them playing on some of the finest links courses in Ireland, I am again hopeful that, like in Ballybunnion, their aim is good as I'm sure being hit by a stray golf ball is not a pleasant thing for a motorcyclist.

I stop briefly at Liscannor to admire the small harbour and its view back over towards the coast and towns that I had just travelled. The harbour and town are overlooked by the ruins of Liscannor Castle from which the town gets its name. *Lios Ceannuir*, meaning O'Connor's Fort, was a stronghold of the O'Connor family who were once dominant in

Liscannor Harbour

this area. Liscannor is also the birthplace of John P. Holland, who is credited with inventing the submarine. Though he is not buried here, a headstone beside the church commemorates his career and the nearby Holland Street is named in his honour.

Leaving Liscannor I noticed a prominent pillar in the distance and my curious eye was drawn to it. It turned out to be a memorial to Cornelius O'Brien, a local Member of Parliament who died in 1857. The date on the pillar is 1853 and is regarded as a 'typo' since he was clearly still alive. He is remembered on the pillar as someone who laboured to 'promote the prosperity of his country and the happiness and comfort of his people'. The memorial is signed by one Colman M. O'Lochlen. I have already seen this surname, and variations of its spelling including my own, several times today. The pillar is beside St Bridget's Well, a place of pilgrimage where people leave offerings such as memorial cards and prayerful messages on the walls of the well.

Monument to Cornelius O'Brien

I am now getting closer to the Cliffs of Moher, which are often regarded as one of the great natural wonders of the world. You need to be prepared to have your breath taken away by the magnificent cliff faces. The road gets noticeably busier and when I arrived on site I was directed to a car park on the other side of the road along with hundreds of cars. There was no special place to park a motorcycle and I saw no others there. All my luggage was on the bike and I didn't fancy carrying everything over to the Cliffs. A kind car park attendant offered to 'keep an eye' on the bike for me. This

St Bridget's Well, Liscannor

is one of the busiest spots in Clare with over a million people a year visiting one of Ireland's best known natural attractions. I was here before, in 1985, and the site is much changed with shops and an Interpretative Centre embedded into the hill near the cliffs. I think this is tastefully done and does not detract from the location.

I heard a lot of non-English-speaking tourists who were wandering around the many paths here. French seemed to me to be the most common language being spoken; *oh là là* as they gazed at the cliffs. A young couple in their wedding outfit attracted much attention. They were sure lucky with their wedding day; it could have been yesterday in the rain when they would surely have been blown off the cliffs. There were also a good few buskers – a lady with a harp was brilliant, and another with a concertina was dreadful. Much has been written about the Cliffs themselves, and they have even appeared on film as a backdrop for movies like *Harry Potter and the Half Blood Prince* and *Ryan's Daughter*. Like everyone else there I drink in the sights of the majestic

Cliffs of Moher

cliffs. They are 214 metres high at the highest point, and range for 8 kilometres along the coast. They are made up of layer upon layer of hardened sand, silt and mud, and are home to an estimated 30,000 birds. O'Brien's Tower overlooking the cliffs is named after Cornelius O'Brien mentioned above. Apparently he was involved in developing this location as a tourist attraction. I stayed a long time looking out to sea and pondered on my travels so far. I'm right on the edge of the coast on a beautiful Irish summer's day having travelled almost half-way around the Wild Atlantic Way. It is a good feeling.

Having been blown away by the Cliffs, the equally majestic Burren landscape was next. The coast road from the Cliffs of Moher up to Black Head is about 28 kilometres long and must be one of the most spectacular rides in Ireland as it circles around the Burren. To my left is the Atlantic Ocean with views out to the Aran Islands and across Galway Bay to Connemara, while to my right are the marvels of limestone rock formations. Approaching Doolin I noticed a wonderful looking round tower castle on high ground. This is Doonagore Castle which was built in the sixteenth century. You cannot visit the castle as it is now a private home. From the village of Doolin I rode down to the port from where you can get a ferry to the Aran Islands, and where in the distance you can still see the Cliffs of Moher to the south.

The Burren is a unique habitat with rare plants that attract botanists from all over the world. The limestone that makes up the Burren

O'Brien's Castle at the Cliffs of Moher

is called karst, and is one of the largest and best examples of this type of rock formation in Europe. In geological terms, the Burren is quite young with the karst being dated to 10,000 years ago. The road from the Cliffs of Moher through the village of Doolin is situated away from the coast for a while, but returns to a coast road at a place called Ailladie where I stop for a walk over the limestone. This is regarded as one of Ireland's best rock-climbing locations. It is also a popular stopping point for tourists where they can get up close to the limestone rocks and the view out to the Aran Islands. I too stopped and went down to the small cliffs here to stand at the edge, something you are not allowed to do back at the Cliffs of Moher. I got a fellow tourist to take a photo of me looking out to sea. If it wasn't for their higher cousins back down the road, the small cliffs here would themselves be a major tourist attraction. All along this road there are cars parked at the side of the road, their owners and passengers enjoying the walk over the rocks.

Standing on the edge of the Wild Atlantic Way in Ailladie

The cliffs at Ailladie

One of the few beaches in this area is at Fanore where the caravan and mobile home park has the beautiful limestone Slieve Elva as a backdrop. At Black Head I look out over Galway Bay to what must be one of the smallest lighthouses in Ireland, though it's of interest because its light is fuelled by solar power. Behind me is Gleninagh Mountain and I wonder if there is a more beautiful place in Ireland than right here?

The astute reader will notice that I have not mentioned Oliver Cromwell, who I seem to be following around Ireland, in some time. Indeed, he had returned to England while his troops continued his campaign against the Irish in County Clare. By then his army was commanded by General Edmund Ludlow, who was clearly not as impressed by the Burren as I was. He is quoted as having said this about the Burren: 'Not a tree whereon to hang a man; no water in which to drown him; no soil in which to bury him.' Ludlow is perhaps more famous for being regarded as a regicide since he was one of the judges that condemned King Charles I of England to death.

One of the things that attracts people to different parts of Ireland is the search for ancestors, and I am no different. North Clare is O'Loughlin country, and for a short time I travelled the Wild Atlantic Way in search of my own ancestors. A short distance after Black Head I stopped at the side of the road to look down at a castle which is visible for a long way along the beautiful ride on the southern side of Galway Bay. It is the sixteenth century Gleninagh Castle and it was built for the O'Loughlin chiefs who were resident there up to the 1840s. It was lived in up to the 1890s, but is still well preserved. I wondered if any of my direct ancestors had lived there. There is no shortage of people with the O'Loughlin name in County Clare, and this northern region of the county is where the name O'Loughlin originates from. At the end

Towards Black Head on the edge of the Burren

O'Loughlin's Pub, Ballyvaughan

of the tenth century some of the Irish upper classes started to adopt Viking names such as *Lochlainn,* and it is thought that some of the County Clare families did so as well. The Vikings were known as *na Lochlannaigh* in the Irish language. My dad Joe has told me that his grandfather, also Joe O'Loughlin, was born and reared in County Clare, but he does not know which part. It could be that the O'Loughlins are descended from either the Vikings themselves, or from a County Clare family that adopted the name.

I stopped in Ballyvaughan for petrol, and also to check out O'Loughlin's pub as it was lunchtime. Sadly it was closed and not opening until eight o'clock in the evening. I noticed a sign over the door for 'O'Loughlin's Whiskey', which I had never heard of before. I felt like I was in some sort of O'Loughlin heaven having just seen a castle, a pub and now a whiskey with my surname – all within a

Shanmuckinish Castle, near Ballyvaughan

few minutes. The village of Ballyvaughan also once had a castle that the O'Loughlin family lived in, but by the mid-nineteenth century the castle was in ruins and only the foundations remain today.

The O'Loughlins must have been good castle builders because shortly after leaving Ballyvaughan I spot the tower house-shaped Shanmuckinish castle located right on the edge of the sea. From a distance it looks intact, but only one side of it stands while the rest has fallen into ruin. This castle is thought to date from the sixteenth century and one of its residents was the curiously named Mcloughlin O'Loughlin. The O'Loughlin family were once one of the most powerful families in this part of north County Clare. The head of the family was often referred to as the King or Prince of the Burren. There is evidence of this at Corcomroe Abbey to which I take a short detour from the coast road at Bell Harbour. The abbey was built in the thirteenth century by the Cistercians on the instructions of King Conor na Siudane Ua Briain, who died in battle in 1267 and is reputedly buried in the abbey. Legend has it that he had the five stonemasons who built the abbey killed to prevent them from replicating it elsewhere. The abbey was lived in by the Cistercians until the mid-seventeenth century. The floor of the abbey contains many graves, including one with the inscription 'O'Loughlin King of Burren's Family Tomb'. While I have no idea if I am of royal descent, or descended from the O'Loughlins buried here, I feel a certain respect as if I was standing beside the grave of a close relative. All along the Wild Atlantic Way there may be many opportunities for the tourist to check out family history and the origins of their family name. My ancestors who lived here probably travelled about by horse, and as I rode through North Clare on my iron horse, I felt a special connection with this land of my ancestors.

My final port of call in County Clare is to the romantically named Flaggy Shore near New Quay. Here you can see exposed limestone rock formations on the nearby hill that continue down to the shore. The strange grey beauty here caught the imagination of Nobel Laureate

Seamus Heaney who loved North Clare and spent many holidays there. In one of his most famous poems, 'Postscript', he acclaims the Flaggy Shore which will 'catch the heart off guard and blow it open'. I rode right along the shore and around the small Lough Murree, through Finavarra and the rest of this beautiful land that has inspired poets and artists for centuries. The Flaggy Shore was my last stop in Clare as it is close to the county boundary with Galway. It is still just mid-afternoon and I had travelled the entire 210 kilometres of the County Clare coast in around seven hours. After having taken several days to get around counties Cork and Kerry, I felt that Clare had passed by in a heartbeat. But I leave Clare having enjoyed its unique landscape that certainly lives up to the name of the Wild Atlantic Way.

Another view of Ailladie

4

GALWAY – INTO THE WEST

I crossed into the county of Galway and the province of Connaught with Oliver Cromwell's 'To Hell or to Connaught' quote in my mind. He famously offered the native Irish this choice when he was busy confiscating as much land as possible in the rest of Ireland for his own soldiers and supporters. At least in Connaught I hope to get away from Cromwell for a while. For me there are no thoughts of hell today as I ride on to Galway and into the heart of the West. From Kinvara Bay at the start of County Galway, to Killary Harbour at the end, the coastline is an endless combination of bays, inlets, peninsulas, islands and headlands.

The first stop in Galway is at Traught Beach, which is reached over a short causeway on the western edge of Kinvarra Bay at the end of which there is a ruin of a windmill like round tower. This beach offers nice views over Galway Bay and to the city of Galway in the distance. The first village I encounter in County Galway is Kinvara into which I arrive in glorious sunshine. Kinvara is a popular fishing village with a long tradition of trading along the Clare and Galway coastlines. Every August, the village celebrates this tradition with the *Cruinniú na mBád* ('Gathering of the Boats') festival where turf boats, known as Galway Hookers, gather for a weekend of racing, celebration, and no doubt some craic. I took a brief stop at the small harbour but it was

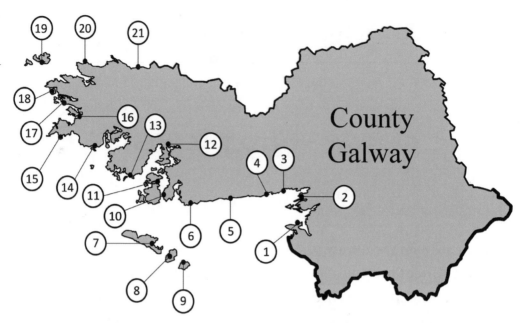

Wild Atlantic Way
342 Kilometres

Wild Atlantic Way – Galway Discovery Points

1. Traught Beach	2. Rinville Park	3. Salthill Promenade
4. Silver Strand	5. Spiddal	6. Ceiba an Tsruthain
7. Inis Mór	8. Inis Meain	9. Inis Oirr
10. Trá Geal	11. Lettermore Causeway	12. Gortmore
13. Finish Island	14. Gorteen Bay	15. Bunowen Bay
16. Derrygimla	17. Sky Road	18. Omey Island
19. Inishbofin	20. Crump Island View	21. Killary Harbour (South)

empty of Galway Hookers today. I imagined it full of these majestic boats decorating the bay with their traditional black hulls and dark, red-brown sails. Just past Kinvara is the equally majestic Dunguaire Castle which dominates this remote edge of Galway Bay. This restored tower castle with surrounding walls is open to the public and is thought to be one of the most photographed castles in Ireland. It dates from around 1520 and was once owned by the writer Oliver St John Gogarty, who established it as a meeting place for other writers such as W.B. Yeats, George Bernard Shaw, Lady Gregory and J.M. Synge. During the summer there are medieval banquets every night, and I can't help but imagine that it would be brilliant to be sitting at a table chatting with such greats of Irish literature.

Local legend has it that if you stand at the gates of Dunguaire Castle and ask a question, that you will get an answer before the end of the day. As it was now well into the afternoon I was ready for a late lunch and I

Dunguaire Castle

Moran's of the Weir

asked myself where would I go? Back on the bike I kept an eye out for a likely place, but when I saw signs for Kilcolgan and Clarinbridge my question was answered. This is the location for the well-known restau-

... And their famous oysters

rant and bar, Moran's of the Weir, which was first established in 1797. It is located on the banks of the Kilcolgan River as it meanders towards Galway Bay. There are many people sitting outside having lunch, and no doubt they heard my bike coming from a long way off in this beautiful and quiet location. This locality is host to the famous Clarinbridge Oyster Festival that has been running here every year in September since 1954, with locally produced oysters at the heart of events. Moran's is famous for its oysters and I had a dozen with delicious brown bread. I'd love to have washed them down with a pint of Guinness, but a pot of tea had to do. Delicious, and for the second time on this trip I was also able to eat outside looking out over the river. I ordered a second pot of tea and checked on the photos of the wonderful Clare coastline that I had taken so far today. I also studied my maps to plan the rest of the day and decided to aim for the western side of Galway city with a target of reaching Spiddal.

Back on the main road riding towards Galway I took the short road down to Rinville Park, which surrounds a magnificent sixteenth century estate. It has many paths and trails, and is a popular place for a day out for the people of Galway city. I also rode down to Rinville pier to see the full view of Galway Bay to the west. I can imagine it being a popular place to watch the sun setting over the bay.

For the first time on this journey I enjoyed a bit of speed on the dual-carriageway between Oranmore and Galway. I had planned to go past the city since it was quiet coastal roads that I wanted to ride. But Galway does not have a bypass, so I went into the city centre and parked in a pedestrian area outside the Skeffington Arms Hotel on Eyre Square. Galway is known as the 'City of the Tribes', a nickname that comes from the fourteen tribes, or families, who dominated the business, political and social life in Galway up to the late nineteenth century. People who live in Galway are often referred to today as the 'tribesmen'. On Eyre Square there are flags displayed to represent each of the fourteen tribes.

It was almost six o'clock in the evening when I set out on a walk around the compact city centre. I walked through the busy pedestrianised Shop Street where buskers were entertaining both shoppers and the many tourists like me. About half way down the street is Lynch's Castle, which is thought to be the finest surviving town castle in Ireland. Look out for the row of gargoyles near the top of the walls as they are a rare sight in Ireland. The castle was built in the late fifteenth century and it is in use today as a bank. The Lynch family who lived there also have another claim to fame. At the time the castle was built, one of the Lynch family was Mayor of Galway, but his son was convicted of the murder of a Spanish sailor and sentenced to death. Nobody would hang him, so his father did the deed himself from a window. The word 'lynching', to denote illegal vigilante style hangings, may have originated from this story.

Shop Street continues on into the narrow Quay Street which has many cafés, pubs and restaurants. At the end of Quay Street you can walk around to the famous Spanish Arch, an area now known in Galway as the 'Latin Quarter'. The Arch was built in 1584 and stands on the left bank of the River Corrib. It was once part of the city walls and was damaged during the 1755 tsunami which was caused by an earthquake in far-away Lisbon. Directly across the river from the Spanish Arch is the area known as The Claddagh, which gives its name to the well-known Claddagh ring that is worn as a symbol of love, loyalty and friendship.

Returning to the bike I headed out to a very busy Salthill where there were hundreds of people enjoying the evening sunshine. I stopped for a few minutes by the promenade which is about 3 kilometres long. I have walked this promenade many times before and enjoyed the contrast between one side full of restaurants, bars, hotels and entertainment centres, and on the other side the beautiful Galway Bay with the Clare coastline clearly visible in the distance. Despite complaining about the weather all the time, all it takes is for the sun to shine for a short while to make Irish people happy.

I motor on through the busy village of Bearna, which marks the beginning of Connemara. Nobody seems to know exactly what area makes up Connemara, but most agree that it consists of the county of Galway west of Lough Corrib, plus some parts of south Mayo. Oscar Wilde once said that 'Connemara is a savage beauty', and by the time I left this beautiful land I was in complete agreement with him. Much of

Salthill

the region is Irish-speaking, and the pupils of the many Gaeltacht summer schools in this area are out in force like teenage gangs on holiday. Close to Bearna is Silver Strand, which is a lovely beach in the midst of rocks and a dramatic eroded small headland. This shows the power of the sea as if the headland was chopped off by a large wave.

Reaching Spiddal I pulled up outside the An Crúiscín Lán hotel hoping to find accommodation, again with a handy bar downstairs, but unfortunately there was no room at the inn. The barman recommended I try the road out of the village where I found a room at the very comfortable Cala nUisce bed and breakfast run by the wonderfully chatty Moya. Once settled in I walked back towards the village and took a short tour on foot around the harbour area. The road down to the harbour is dominated by the gothic-style church, which is regarded as a

An Crúiscín Lán hotel

masterpiece of modern church architecture and art. The nearby small harbour looks great in the evening sunshine and I sat on a rock on the shore trying to remember the words of the famous song 'Galway Bay', but all I could recall was 'see the sun go down on Galway Bay'.

Further along the harbour there is a stone dedicated to three men: Ruaidhrí Ó Flaitheartaigh, Eoghan Ó Neachtain and Mártín Ó Cadhain. The stone reads in Irish *Laochra litriochta agus Béaloidis an cheantair* ('literature and folklore heroes of the area', according to my basic Irish). Ó Flaitheartaigh was a historian and the last Lord of *Iar Connacht* (another name for Connemara). He published one of the earliest histories of Ireland, called *Ogygia*, in 1685. He was the last Lord of this region because (who else) Oliver Cromwell confiscated his lands in the 1650s. Maybe Cromwell also wanted a bit of 'hell'? Eoghan Ó Neachtain was a playwright known for the Irish play *An Liúdramán'* (*The Drone*). This play title is often used as an insult and is sometimes

Spiddal Harbour

abbreviated to *liúdar*. Mártín Ó Cadhain, who was born in Spiddal, was one of the most prominent writers in Irish of the last century. The An Crúiscín Lán hotel is my final port of call for the day where I enjoyed a pint and delicious burger and fries. The name of the hotel translates from Irish as 'The Little Full Jug', and I felt full after a great day's riding. The weather forecast for the next two days predicted good riding conditions, so I hoped I would have another great day exploring the ins and outs of Galway.

On a glorious morning I set out west from Spiddal into Connemara. The fine day made this one of the best days on the road so far. There are great views of the islands and North Clare all along this Connemara coast road. If you look at a map of this road you will see lanes to the left down to the sea, and lanes to the right up into the hills; it looks like a fish-bone diagram. On one of these roads I rode down towards the sea to Ceiba an Tsruthain to a small pier and viewing area that looks out over North Clare and the Aran Islands. A feature of the rugged landscape here are the number of stone walls that mark out the numerous small fields. In Rossaveel I called down to the harbour which was busy with people getting the ferry to the Aran Islands for the day. I have been to the islands before where I enjoyed a pony and trap ride around Inishmore to the ruins at Dún Aonghus, which is a prehistoric fort situated at the edge of a 100 metre high cliff. I was tempted to go again today, but narrow roads, ponies and a Harley-Davidson motorcycle do not make for a great mix. Rossaveel is also a large fishing port and already there were fishermen gutting fish caught in the early morning. These fish guts were obviously a feast for the noisy and grateful seagulls who were having breakfast in the harbour courtesy of the fishermen.

Back on the main road and just before the village of Casla is the location of Costelloe Lodge which has an interesting history. It is a private house on a slight detour, but is not visible from the road. Nevertheless it is interesting to think that J. Bruce Ismay, chairman of the

Rossaveel Harbour

View of Costelloe over Casla Bay

White Star Line that built the *Titanic* liner, lived in the Lodge during the 1920s and 1930s. Along with the three women who I saw commemorated in Ballydehob a few days ago, he survived the sinking of the *Titanic*. He bought the Lodge in order to escape the ridicule of survival as a man despite the 'women and children first' lifeboat policy as the *Titanic* sank. The *Titanic* was a forbidden topic of discussion in the Lodge. Local Irish-speaking neighbours are reputed to have referred to him in Irish as *Brú síos mé* ('lower me down'), as into a lifeboat.

I stopped just outside Casla for a map check as the Wild Atlantic Way zig-zags quite a bit in this region. This is the beginning of some riding through islands and around bays that I had never visited before. Villages and towns like Casla, Carraroe, Lettermore and Lettermullan are very close to each other. The roads are quite good and I enjoyed riding through this remote part of Connemara. There are rocks everywhere, sticking out like bald heads through the grass. I first ride through Carraroe, whose Irish name is *An Cheathrú Rua,* which means a red and rugged area. At the end of the peninsula here is *Trá Geal,* where you will also find a beach with a small stone monument marking *Trá na bPáistí* ('the Children's Beach'), so named because there is a burial ground for unbaptised children nearby.

I looped back around the Carraroe peninsula to Bealadangan where I stopped to view the calm waters of Greatman's Bay. The islands of Lettermore, Gorumna and Lettermullan are linked with narrow causeways and I have to slow down to navigate the increasingly narrow twisty lanes. I didn't know what was ahead of me as I passed through Lettermore Island, the first of the three islands on this road. Riding through Gorumna Island and on to Lettermullen Island I was surrounded by fantastic rugged scenery. The Wild Atlantic Way stops at the Lettermore Causeway, but it is well worth continuing on for a short trip down to Golam Head.

Right in the middle of what I perceived to be nowhere, I saw a sign for a heritage centre and my first reaction was that someone was making a joke. Nevertheless, I decided to check it out and it turned out to be the very real and delightful Lettermullen and Gorumna Heritage Centre. This is what makes the Wild Atlantic Way special for me: finding little gems like this in the most unexpected places. Local historian John Bhaba Jeaic Ó Confhaola was a collector of old books in Irish and English, as well as newspapers and magazines from times past. There are lots of tools, traditional items, books, photos, medals and typewriters. I picked up a copy of the *Irish Independent* dated Monday 25 November 1963, which had the headline 'Kennedy Suspect Shot' and featured the iconic photograph of Lee Harvey Oswald cringing as he is being shot by Jack Ruby. My earliest memory is of two days earlier when President John F. Kennedy was assassinated, allegedly by Oswald. This is a real hidden treasure trove that is well worth a visit. I got talking to the attendants who told me that they were scanning a lot of the material to make it available to researchers. They also told me to be sure and ride

*Inside the Lettermullen and Gorumna Heritage Centre (top)
and the iconic newspaper*

Causeway near Golam Head

down the lane a bit further to see one of the few remaining Lloyd's Towers in Ireland at the tip of Golam Head.

Ten of these towers were built in the early nineteenth century to warn of any invasion by Napoleon, the west coast equivalent of Martello Towers. They were also used to keep an eye out for smugglers. I got off the bike and stood in admiration of the tower and surrounding landscape. This is truly one of the most peaceful places I have ever been, and I fill my lungs with the cleanest air in Europe. This peace and clean air did not last long as a car with four occupants pulled up beside the bike. To my amazement they stayed inside the car, rolled down their windows a few centimetres, and lit up cigarettes! I left them there with smoke billowing out of their windows and retraced my route back along the road through the three islands to Bealadangan.

Next I ride around Camus Bay towards Gortmore and Ros Muc. As a former marine biologist I would love to have spent some time exploring the sheltered shores of this bay for marine wildlife. There are also a lot of small freshwater lakes in this region, which combined with its geology is a scientist's paradise. Ros Muc is at the end of a small peninsula and my first stop is at the holiday cottage of one of the area's most famous former residents, revolutionary and educator Patrick Pearse. His actions in Easter week 1916 are well-known, but perhaps less known is his lifetime devotion to education. He was particularly interested in teaching in a bilingual environment, and studied this in detail in the bilingual societies of Belgium and Wales.

In 1905 he bought a plot of land in Ros Muc overlooking Lough Eiliarach, and later built the cottage in Irish vernacular style with a thatched roof. From 1909 he used it as both a holiday home and as a

Inside Pearse's Cottage

Gaeltacht summer school for his pupils. The location is quite remote and must have given him solace from his debts in Dublin. To me it is a spartan cottage with few comforts, though it is clear that Pearse did not have much money. I got talking to the Office of Public Works guide at the cottage who told me that it was here where Pearse wrote one of his most famous speeches which he delivered as an oration at the graveside of the well-known Fenian Jeremiah O'Donovan Rossa in 1915. Pearse's fellow revolutionary, Tom Clarke, told him to make the speech 'as hot as hell'. This he did when ending his oration with the fiery lines: 'But the fools, the fools, the fools! – they have left us our Fenian dead, and while Ireland holds these graves, Ireland unfree shall never be in peace.' The cottage is quite simple and it does not take long to view it, but it is a must for any student of Irish history.

Moving on, I set out for Carna, Roundstone and Ballyconneely. For kilometre after kilometre the countryside here is rugged, with little or no tillage. There are lots of rocks and stone walls about, and my pace is pleasantly slow; it's impossible to tire of this scenery. A new *ohrwurm* enters my head, 'Wild Thing' by The Troggs, which is fitting

View of the Twelve Pins over Bertraghboy Bay

Roundstone

for this wild landscape. The countryside here is all about scenery, and on this beautiful day I am enjoying the wild landscape of Connemara. The mad world of recession, depression and austerity seems a million miles away. Close to Carna is the long and narrow Finish Island which can be reached on foot during low tides. Nearby is Mweenish Island which is connected to the mainland by narrow roads across the rocky shore. From here there are excellent views back towards Finish Island and to the Lettermullan and Gorumna islands I visited earlier. Mweenish Island was once was well known for the building of the traditional Galway Hooker sailing boat.

Near Glinsk I stop at the edge of Bertraghboy Bay and am greeted with a breathtaking view of the Twelve Bens (or Pins) mountains in the distance. This is a group of twelve mountains which are popular with walking and climbing enthusiasts, and are the dominant feature of this part of Connemara. I took my time riding around Bertraghboy Bay and its many sheltered inlets. At Roundstone I stop at the small harbour and take some photos in one of the oldest fishing villages on the west coast. In the village I noticed an archway to the left and rode down to investigate. It turned out to be part of a Franciscan monastery dating from 1835, but which was closed in the 1970s. Today, this archway and a beautiful bell tower are all that's left of the monastery; the site is now called Michael Killeen Park. It is home to the Roundstone Music and Craft Shop which is owned and managed by Malachy Kearns, who is Ireland's only full-time bodhrán maker. Here you can see how bodhráns are made out of goat skin in the traditional manner. Roundstone is well known for its arts and culture. Famous painters such as Paul Henry and Jack B. Yeats painted here, and it is not difficult to see why they chose this area. A little further on past Roundstone are the side-by-side beaches at Gorteen Bay and Dog's Bay. The whiteness of the sand here is rare in Ireland, and there were several families out enjoying the crystal clear water.

Just before Ballyconneely I turned off for Slyne Head where the landscape changes a bit from stony fields to sandy dunes. On the way to the head I noticed the ruins of an early sixteenth century castle at Bunowen. This was reputedly home to the O'Flaherty family, one of whom, Donall, married the celebrated 'Pirate Queen' Grace O'Malley (or Granuaile) in 1546. They raised a family here until Donall was killed, and she moved to Mayo where I would come across her legacy again. The castle fell into ruin in the nineteenth century and today stands like a gothic shadow on the horizon which would not look out of place in a Dracula movie.

I stopped for a map check at the pier in Bunowen Bay where there is another beautiful white sandy beach. I had the pier to myself and I enjoyed the flat blue sea and clear sky; a little bit of summer on one of the most western parts of Ireland. The road does not quite go as far as

Bunowen Castle

Slyne Head, which is in fact on a small island. This is a smashing location for the Connemara Golf Club, plus many mobile homes. You can't get down to the Head as the land is private, and there is even a 'Beware of the Bull' sign to keep the nearby campers and touring bikers out.

The landscape around Ballyconneely is a beautiful mix of bogs, lakes and rocks. It was here in 1854 that the first salmon farming operation in Ireland was set up in the clean waters off shore. But Ballyconneely is more famous for the events of Sunday, 15 June 1919. It was on this day that Captain John Alcock and Lieutenant Arthur Whitten-Brown ended the first non-stop transatlantic flight from Newfoundland in Canada to Derrygimla Bog about 5 kilometres north of Ballyconneely. They landed their twin engine *Vickers Vimy* plane after 16 hours and 27 minutes of flight at an average speed of 184 kilometres per hour. There are two sites commemorating this event. The first is a stone monument, dedicated in 1959, in the shape of a tail fin from an airplane

Alcock and Brown Memorial at Ballinaboy

situated on a lane to the left of the main road at Ballinaboy. This is a curious shape as it looks like a more modern jet tail fin, and is not in the least similar to the tail fin of the *Vickers Vimy* that Alcock and Brown flew. It overlooks the second site, where the actual landing took place, which is a few hundred metres on the other side of the main road.

I rode down a lane with a dreadful surface to see a white concrete cairn that points out the landing spot. The lane was a real test of my riding skills and after a while I began to wonder if I was on the right track as there was no sign of anything other than turf and stones. At the end of the lane the concrete cairn is located beside the ruins of a Marconi wireless telegraphy station; nothing more than the foundations of the station are left. It was from here that the first transatlantic radio-telegraph service was launched in 1907 between Ireland and Nova Scotia in Canada. Just like at Valentia Island earlier in my journey, I wondered at the technological skills of the early pioneers of communication, and what they would have thought of satellites and mobile phones. At one stage over 400 people were employed at the station, including Jack Phillips who was later to become the chief radio operator on board the *Titanic*. Unlike J. Bruce Esmay and the three ladies from Ballydehob, Phillips perished when the *Titanic* sunk on 15 April 1912. The station was burned down during the Civil War in 1922 and never rebuilt.

I rode on towards Clifden, which is sometimes referred to as the capital of Connemara, and it was certainly as busy as a capital city today with lots of people about. It is situated in the middle of some of the wildest and most imposing scenery that Connemara has to offer on the Wild Atlantic Way. It was also crowded with cars and it was difficult to find a place to park the bike on the hilly main street where I stopped for a coffee at Walsh's Bakery. The town has had a chequered history with a lot of conflict between landlords and the local population. In 1843 Daniel O'Connell held a monster meeting here in front of a crowd of reputedly

Ruins of a Marconi wireless station and cairn
marking the place near where Alcock and Brown landed

Clifden

over 100,000 people. There is an old joke that O'Connell addressed the crowd speaking in English but that nobody could understand him. A hundred years later former President of Ireland Éamon de Valera addressed a mass meeting in Clifden, spoke in Irish and nobody could understand him! Clifden suffered badly during the Great Famine of 1845, with death from starvation and emigration decimating the local population. The town was also severely damaged during the War of Independence when the Black and Tans terrorised the townspeople and set fire to many houses.

At Clifden there is a great 11 kilometre ride around a small peninsula called the Sky Road from which there are uninterrupted views of the Atlantic from the southern side, and of Streamstown Bay on the northern side. I rode along the other side of Streamstown Bay to the interesting

Omey Island, which is a flat tidal island that can be reached by walking or driving over the large sandy strand. I did not for a moment consider taking my motorcycle over the strand, but judging by the tracks in the sand, some drivers had already crossed over to the island, which is known for its holy well and has a small lake at its centre.

A short distance away is the village of Cleggan. There is a small harbour here which was crowded with cars, no doubt belonging to people who had taken the ferry to Inishbofin Island for the day, and even on a motorcycle I found it hard to find a place to park. At the end of the pier is a wonderful and touching poem carved in granite which is dedicated to a man called Desmond. He died at sea near here in 2002, but according to the poem, 'He would leave Cleggan Pier in the early morn, smiling and always in great form'. This is also the location of a terrible tragedy in 1927 when 25 fishermen from the local area drowned during a storm. This left the area devastated as so many breadwinners were lost in what became known as the Cleggan Bay Disaster. Chastened

The harbour at Cleggan

On the Connemara Loop

once again by the power of the sea I ride away from Cleggan and set off back towards Letterfrack through bog lined roads and some small forests.

Letterfrack is smaller than it appears on my map. It is a village that was founded by the Quakers after the Great Famine in 1849. The Quakers helped with the post-famine relief effort and founded a school and some small businesses. Like Clifden, Letterfrack also had a Marconi station which operated here from 1913 to 1922 when it was closed after the fire at the Clifden station. Today Letterfrack is better known for the Connemara National Park Visitor Centre which tells us that the park was set up in 1980 and consists of 2,957 hectares of mountains, bogs and woods. It is mostly made up of the lands which formed part of the now infamous Letterfrack Industrial School and the nearby Kylemore

Abbey estate. Indeed, the Centre itself was formerly part of the school. Letterfrack is also located on the Connemara Loop, which is a trail that is 80 kilometres long. It is mostly an inland trail, but I ride along this part of it towards Renvyle. On the way I stop at Tully Cross where I noticed a replica wooden Viking longboat at the side of the road beside Paddy Coyne's Pub.

At the end of this road are the ruins of Renvyle Castle where I stopped to take in the wonderful setting, especially the view out to Crump Island. There's no doubt that the folks who built castles always seem to have chosen the best locations. Here I listened to an old man describing the history of the castle to a group of young people. He told us that this castle was first built in the thirteenth century and is also reputed to have been the home of Grace O'Malley and Donall O'Flaherty (who we met earlier in Bunowen). Legend also had it that the castle originally belonged to the Joyce clan but was taken over by the O'Flahertys after a massacre at a wedding where all but one of the

Replica wooden Viking longboat

Renvyle Castle

Joyce family were killed. Close to the castle is the well-known Renvyle House Hotel, which I remember in the past as advertising itself as Ireland's only 'stress-free zone'. The original house here once belonged to the writer Oliver St John Gogarty. In the distance to the north I could see Connaught's highest mountain, Mweelrea. At 814 metres high it dominates the region and provides a wonderful backdrop to this peaceful place. There is no stress here, but I have to move on. It is late afternoon and I need to make it as far as Westport in County Mayo this evening where I planned to stay with my in-laws.

For the next 50 kilometres or so I am diverted away from the coast and ride inland. The landscape changes briefly from bogs and stones to lakes and tree-lined roads. At Kylemore Lough I watch out for the famous Abbey of the same name, but this is a popular tourist attraction and I have to watch the road carefully due to a lot of traffic. The thought struck me that others might be trying to do the same thing as me, that is, look at the wonderful scenery and drive at the same time on narrow roads.

Kylemore Abbey is a true hidden gem in a picturesque hill and lakeside setting. It was originally built as a private home by Mitchell Henry starting in 1867. To get an indication of its size, it had over 70 rooms and took 100 men four years to complete. In 1920 the Benedictine nuns, who fled from Belgium after World War I, set up a school for girls which was eventually closed in 2010. The large Victorian walled garden is six acres in size and is a popular tourist destination today. Leaving the Kylemore Abbey area, the road once again runs through bog land with very few trees. Though the area is thinly populated and a bit bleak, the setting is magnificent as there are mountains and hills a short distance away on both sides of the road.

The final part of my ride around the Galway coast led me to Killary Harbour, a fjord-shaped, deep water inlet. In the early evening sunshine I stopped on a hill above the harbour beside the Killary Harbour Adventure Centre to gaze down on the still waters and high hills that make this a very dramatic environment. In my scuba diving days I dived the harbour several times and remember clear water full of sea life. The harbour is 16 kilometres long and is 45 metres deep in places. It is also a centre for aquaculture with a lot of salmon and mussels farmed here. The road runs alongside the harbour until it reaches the village of Leenaun. I parked the bike at the edge of the village and tried to get some professional looking photos of my bike and long evening shadows with the harbour and mountains as a backdrop. There is no doubt that this is one of the most beautiful places in Galway, and I feel as though the best has been kept to last for me.

After Leenaun, the road continues along the narrowing harbour until I eventually arrive at the sign welcoming me to County Mayo. I had journeyed over 342 kilometres of roads ranging from a dual-carriageway to country lanes. I enjoyed the sights and scenery that this rugged county has to offer over two days of brilliant riding. This part of the Wild Atlantic Way is a journey in itself. You know that if you are sad to leave a place that you must have enjoyed it, but it was time to leave the land of 'savage beauty' behind.

Evening in Leenaun at Killary Harbour

5

MAYO – THE 'MIGHTY' WAY

I t was early evening when I crossed into Mayo, which has some of the most beautiful landscapes in Ireland. It rivals Galway for ruggedness, Clare for cliffs and rock faces, and Kerry for places of interest. It is also a large county and I would need almost three days to ride around the lengthy coastline. However, at the beginning there are just a few kilometres of Killary Harbour to ride around before the road brought me inland for a considerable distance since the coast around Mweelrea Mountain has no roads.

Mweelrea forms a stunning backdrop overlooking Killary Harbour and I wish I could have taken the bike up to the top for the reported panoramic views over Galway and south Mayo. It is a popular though challenging climb for hill walkers as it is easily accessible with several different ways to get to the top. The name Mweelrea Mountain comes from the Irish *Cnoc Maol Réidh*, which roughly translated means 'bald hill with the smooth top'. Though the road here is not by the sea, I was in for a treat as I passed spectacular lakes and mountain scenery. The route is lined with trees for a while which seemed almost out of place here. Fin Lough, which means 'Bright Lake', is a popular salmon and trout fishing lake. It is also home to Delphi Lodge, which was built at the lakeside in the 1830s by the Marquis of Sligo as a hideaway for the Marquis's hunting and shooting friends. Britain's King Edward

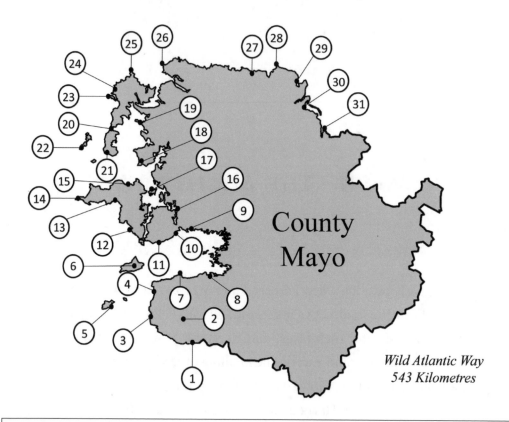

County
Mayo

Wild Atlantic Way
543 Kilometres

Wild Atlantic Way – Mayo Discovery Points

1. *Killary Harbour (North)* 2. *Doo Lough Famine Memorial* 3. *White Strand*

4. *Carrowniskey Strand* 5. *Inishturk* 6. *Clare Island*

7. *Old Head* 8. *Murrisk Viewpoint* 9. *Clew Bay View*

10. *Dooghbeg* 11. *Spanish Armada Viewpoint* 12. *Ashleam Bay*

13. *Keel Beach* 14. *Keem Bay* 15. *Doogort*

16. *Claggan* 17. *Inisbiggle* 18. *Kinrovar*

19. *Claggan Island* 20. *Elly Bay* 21. *Fallmore*

22. *Iniskea South* 23. *Annagh Head* 24. *Doonamo*

25. *Erris Head* 26. *Benwee Head* 27. *Céide Fields*

28. *Downpatrick Head* 29. *Lackan Strand* 30. *Killala Quay*

31. *Ballina Quay*

Killary Harbour North

VII visited the Lodge in 1903, and the future king, Prince Charles, also fished and painted there in 1995.

After just a few kilometres, the trees disappear and the spectacular setting of Doolough Pass comes into view. The road runs right along the edge of Doolough, whose name in Irish means 'Black Lake'. It was on this road that one of the blackest events in Irish history, the Doolough Tragedy, occurred on 31 March 1849 during the Great Famine. Hundreds of starving people were forced to walk 16 kilometres in bad weather from Louisburgh to Delphi Lodge to be inspected as 'paupers' so that they could qualify for famine relief. None was forthcoming and the still starving people had to return home. Nobody knows how many people died on the return journey,

Doo Lough Memorial

though some estimates say over 400 people perished at the side of Doolough. Two memorials commemorate the tragedy. The first is a simple pile of stones at the lakeside road. Further on past the lake is another simple memorial in the form of a cross over-looking Glenullin Lough. It bears a quote from Mahatma Gandhi: 'How can men feel themselves honoured by the humiliation of their fellow beings.' This beautiful location is tinged with tragedy and I can't help thinking how lucky we are today to live in a time of relative plenty, when only a few generations ago our fellow Irish men and women starved to death on this road.

I continued on through blanket bogs and small woodlands as the scenery changed to a flatter landscape. The Tawnymacken Bog National

Heritage Area lies to the west of the road. This is an area of significant conservation value as it in one of the diminishing number of lowland blanket bogs in Europe. This type of habitat is now confined to Britain, Norway, Iceland and Ireland. Just before the location of the bog I turned west towards the tiny village of Killeen. I stopped briefly at the well-preserved Srahmee Megalithic Tomb, which is right beside the road overlooking a small lake. At the end of a long narrow road to the southwest from Killeen you will find the remote and unspoilt White Strand. Heading north along the narrow coast road I stopped briefly at another fine strand at Carrownisky. From here you will have an excellent view out towards both Inishturk and Clare Island. Also visible from many parts of the countryside here is the majestic Croagh Patrick mountain.

Louisburgh is the main town in this region of south Mayo. It was first established in 1795 by the Earl of Altamont as a place of refuge for Catholics fleeing sectarian conflict in Northern Ireland. He named the village after the Battle of Louisburgh, which took place in 1758 during

Clew Bay near Louisburgh

the Seven Years War between the British and the French in Canada. Just after Louisburgh I turn off the main road to Old Head and my first view of Clew Bay. In the distance to the northwest I can see yet another of the many landmarks in this region – Achill Island. I had often heard from local people that Clew Bay was home to 365 islands, one for every day of the year. More informed sources put the figure at 117, many of which are small drumlins. They include Dorinish Island once owned by Beatle John Lennon. While he planned to build a cottage on the island, he never did so. In the early 1970s it was home to a group of hippies for two years. Dorinish Island was meant to be the place where Lennon could get away from all the pressures of his life, but sadly it was not to be. Only sheep and cattle live on the island today, which still gets visits from old hippies and Beatles fans.

Back on the main road again I motor on towards Croagh Patrick, known locally by the affectionate title of the 'Reek'. This is considered

View of Croagh Patrick from Bertra Strand

Famine Ship Memorial in Murrisk

to be the holiest mountain in Ireland, and is a constant presence in the lives of the people of Mayo. Even if it is covered in cloud, they know it is still there. It is famous for an annual pilgrimage to the top of the 'Reek' in honour of St Patrick, who is said to have completed a 40-day Lenten fast and penance on the mountain. Legend also has it that he famously banished all the snakes from Ireland at Croagh Patrick. I have climbed the 'Reek' in the past just once, but it is well worth the effort to get to the top for some spectacular views over Clew Bay. You'll need at least four hours to get to the top and back down again. Across the road from the large car park at the foot of Croagh Patrick is the National Famine Memorial. This fantastic sculpture, created in 1997 to mark the 150th anniversary of the Great Famine, depicts a so-called 'coffin ship' with skeletons scattered across the masts and deck. A short distance behind the memorial is Murrisk Abbey, which was built in 1457 but is now a ruin. It is reputed to have been built on the same site as an original church founded by St Patrick himself. Also close by is the fine long strand called Bertra which juts out into Clew Bay. My day ends in Westport where I spent the evening with family and friends, a relaxed break from bed & breakfast accommodation.

The following morning I wander around Westport, one of Mayo's most popular tourist destinations. Even though it was still early morning, the town was already bustling with tourists and shoppers. In 2012, Westport was voted by *The Irish Times* newspaper as the 'Best Place to Live in Ireland'. I parked at the tree-lined mall and walked up Bridge Street and across Shop Street towards the Octagon at the top of James Street, which features a pillar with a statue of St Patrick on top. Westport is one of the few planned towns in Ireland, and the Octagon is at the heart of the plan created by English architect James Wyatt, who was well known for the design of many great public buildings, churches, houses and gardens in Britain and Ireland in the late eighteenth and early nineteenth centuries. I wished I could stay and enjoy one of the many traditional music sessions found in the numerous pubs, such as at the well-known Matt Molloy's Pub, however it was still early morning and the Wild Atlantic Way was pulling at me to get moving. So I set off for north Mayo, reluctantly leaving Westport behind.

The road from Westport around the eastern and northern sides of Clew Bay runs alongside the 42 kilometre-long Great Western Greenway cycle path. This was one of the first such routes as part of the National Cycle Network. Much of the route uses the old disused Westport to Achill Island railway line, and judging by the number of cyclists it is a very popular amenity. The narrow gauge line was first opened in 1894 and was a social and economic boost to the area in the late nineteenth and early twentieth centuries. However, by the 1930s when roads were being used more, the railway line declined and was eventually closed in 1937. All along the road you will see plenty of small bridges and evidence of where the line ran. One of the best sights is the seven

The Seven Arches bridge in Newport

arch railway viaduct in the town of Newport which spans the Black Oak River. Dominating the town is St Patricks Church, which has special significance for me as I was married to Roma there in 1986. The church is also known for its 'Last Judgement' stained glass windows created by the artist Harry Clarke in what was to be his last work. Newport is also close to the ancestral home of the late Princess Grace of Monaco, and there is a small park in the town named in her honour.

To the north of Newport is the Nephin Beg mountain range, which forms part of the Ballycroy National Park and has one of the largest expanses of blanket bog in Europe. Turning west once again I make a short stop at the ruins of the fifteenth century Dominican Abbey at

Burrishoole, which is located down a narrow lane just outside New-port. The abbey, which was founded in 1470, is situated on raised ground overlooking one of the many small inlets that dot this part of Clew Bay. It was abandoned in 1698 and all that's left today are ruins of the church and cloister. This is a peaceful place, and I am reminded again that some of the best locations around the Wild Atlantic Way are medieval castles and abbeys that today provide tourists with wonderful ruins to visit. Close to Burrishoole Abbey is Carraigahowley Castle, also called Rockfleet Castle, which is a well preserved sixteenth century tower house right on the edge of the Clew Bay shore. The famous 'Pirate Queen' Grace O'Malley (or Granuaile) made this her principal stronghold. According to a sign on the castle, she settled here with 'all her followers and 1,000 head of cows and mares' in her old age. This tower house was one of two such houses built by Granuaile in Mayo that I would come across within hours of each other.

Burrishoole Abbey

Carraigahowley Castle

The road from Newport to Mulranny offers the contrast of the Nephin Beg Mountains on the right and the waters of Clew Bay with views of Clare Island and Croagh Patrick to the left. I stopped at the Mulranny Park Hotel where there is a suite named in honour of John Lennon and Yoko Ono who stayed there in 1968. I sure would like to have been a guest when Lennon performed The Beatles song 'Revolution' to locals and guests at the hotel. Behind the hotel are the remains of a red-bricked railway station beside which is a stop on the Great Western Greenway cycle path. This path continues on to Achill Sound, mostly along the old railway line.

Mulranny is the gateway to the Corraun Peninsula and beyond to Achill Island, and there is a wonderful Atlantic Drive all the way along the edge of Clew Bay. I was now in the Gaeltacht again and wondered what tourists would make of all the *Go Mall* signs in Irish painted on the road. I'm sure that Americans in particular wonder who 'Mall' was,

Old Railway Station, Mulranny

and why the locals are encouraging him to 'Go' all the time! *Go Mall* is, of course, Irish for Go Slow.

There are several places to stop along the road around Corraun, including a memorial to the Spanish Armada. Here there is a plaque to the many ships that were wrecked around the Atlantic coast of Ireland in 1588. Close to this spot was where the 26-gun ship *San Nicolas Prodaneli,* carrying 355 men, was wrecked, and it is thought that only sixteen of the crew survived. Continuing around the Corraun peninsula I rode along Achill Sound which separates Ireland's largest island, Achill, from the mainland. The island is accessed via the whalebone-style Michael Davitt Bridge which was built in 2008. Davitt, one of Mayo's best-known historical figures, was a nationalist, an MP at Westminster and a founder of the Land League.

The village of Achill Sound is also the start of the Achill Atlantic Drive. This is one of the most beautiful coastal drives along the Wild Atlantic Way, especially on a windy day with the sea splashing up on the rocks. The drive continues around the other side of Achill Sound, where there are several interesting sights. First, there is a half statue of Johnny Kilbane across the road from Pattens lounge and bar. Kilbane was born and reared in Cleveland, Ohio, as his father (John) was an emigrant from Achill to America. He was world featherweight champion from 1912 to 1923, which is the second longest reign of a boxing champion, only losing out to the legendary Joe Louis. He later became a state senator in Ohio.

Further along this road are the ruins of Kildownet church, thought to have been built in the 1700s. Though in ruin, there are modern Stations of the Cross located on the internal walls. Beside the church is a cemetery where you will find graves of those who died in several tragedies, including the victims of the Great Famine, a burial plot for 32 victims of a drowning tragedy in Clew Bay in 1894, and the grave of 10 young potato pickers who died in a fire in Scotland in 1937. For the lat-

Kildownet church

ter tragedy, a special train was put on to carry the bodies to Achill just a few weeks before the line was finally closed. Beside Kildownet church is the Achill Island RNLI Lifeboat Station, and Kildownet Castle which was built in the 1400s by Granuaile. It is a well-preserved, narrow tower house about 12 metres high, and was used in the past as a lookout to protect Clew Bay from intruders.

At the southern end of Achill Island is a small island known as Achillbeg, and as you turn north again from there you will be in for a treat as the narrow twisty road runs right along the spectacular rocky coast around Ashleem Bay. In the village of Keel I stop first for a delicious lunch at the Beehive Coffee Shop from which I had spectacular views over Keel beach and beyond to the Minaun Cliffs. The artist Paul Henry is commemorated on a plaque across the road as he lived and worked here from 1910 to 1919. Keel is another of Mayo's popular holiday destinations with the huge sandy beach being a major attraction

Minaun Cliffs

Keem Bay, Achill

Paddle surfers in Keem Bay

for all sorts of sporting activities. There is a single road west from Keel which leads to Keem Bay right at the western end of Achill. The road up and down over the edge of Croaghaun Mountain to Keem is a fantastic approach road with thrilling bends that require you to keep your nerve. Though the road is narrow there are one or two places where you can park as it is a must to stop and view the beach at Keem from a height.

For many years basking sharks were captured here by local fisher-men who extracted valuable oil from the shark's liver. The tactic used to catch the shark was a simple one: a spotter would observe Keem Bay from a height and watch out for the silhouettes and fins of the shark. Once spotted, he called down to men below in the bay who rowed out in currachs to harpoon the unfortunate shark. Much of the oil was ex-tracted from the livers at the nearby Purteen Harbour. Keem was also once the home of Captain Charles Boycott, from whom the English lan-

Horse racing on Keel Strand

guage gets the word 'boycott' following his ostracism by local tenants during a land dispute in 1880. He had a large farm near here and lived in Achill for nearly 20 years before moving to Lough Mask in south Mayo.

Back along the road to Keel to I stopped in the village of Dooagh to see a monument to Don Allum, who in 1987 became the first man to row across the Atlantic in both directions. In 1971 he rowed the Atlantic from east to west, but it was another sixteen years until he completed the second leg from west to east when he landed on the rocky shore at Dooagh in his plywood open boat after 77 days at sea. What a wild way to cross the Atlantic!

One of Achill's best-known attractions is the deserted village on the side of Slievemore Mountain, which is a haunting reminder of past times in this rugged location. The 'village' consists of about 100 ruins of cottages and buildings. It was primarily used for what locals called 'booleying', which was the practice of living in these cottages during the summer months while minding cattle grazing on the mountain. In the winter months the residents returned to their homes in other Achill villages. It is thought that this village was one of the last of its type in Europe. Though the village is not accessible by bike or car, it is easily reached on foot and is a must-see location in Achill.

At the northern side of Achill at the golden strands of Doogort, I got my first sight of Blacksod Bay and a glimpse of the Mullet Peninsula in the distance. This is a much quieter side of Achill and the road winds back towards Achill Sound past the island of Inishbiggle. Back on the Corraun peninsula I rode around the northern side which is less spectacular than the Atlantic Drive on the southern side. Even though it is the middle of summer, the smell of turf fires lends a distinctly west of Ireland feel as I made my way back towards Mulranny.

By now I was riding directly north on a narrow road that cuts through bogs with views towards Claggan Mountain in the east, and back towards Corraun and Achill to the west. After a few kilometres the

Doogort Strand

road turns inland through the small village of Ballycroy and on towards Bangor. The landscape is sparsely populated here and in many places there isn't a house or people to be seen. I really felt close to nature as I rode by flat bog after flat bog. It's almost like riding through a desert, with peat replacing sand. However, soon after crossing the Owenduff River the landscape changes to a mix of bogs and forests. The long straight roads were a pleasure to ride even though this is one of the parts of the Wild Atlantic Way that is furthest from the coast.

At Bangor, a large quarry gives the entrance to the town a 'White Cliffs of Dover' type of look. Bangor is the gateway to Belmullet, but before making my way to this unique peninsula I took a quick detour through the village of Gweesalia, which provided the well-known playwright John Millington Synge with the inspiration for one of his most famous plays, *The Playboy of the Western World*. At Kinrovar Point there is a wonderful view southwards towards the back of Slievemore on Achill Island where I had toured the deserted village earlier. Looking west I could see the end of the Mullet Peninsula which is only about five kilometres away across the calm waters of Blacksod Bay. Later in the day I would be looking from there back to this very place.

On the ride towards the town of Belmullet I stopped briefly at Claggan Island, which is not really an island as it is at the end of a long, thin causeway. The island was formerly the location of the Belmullet Coast Guard, whose building has been converted to a holiday home that offers peace and quiet in a scenic and unspoilt location. Arriving in Belmullet at around 5.30, I decided to arrange accommodation before continuing. I discovered that two weddings in town meant that everywhere was booked out, but one B&B landlady, Mairín, arranged a room for me with her neighbour. It was still early evening so I decided to ride down to Blacksod Point on the one main road that bisects the almost

Blacksod Point Lighthouse

flat Mullet Peninsula. Along the way I enjoyed a pleasant ride listening to the murmur of my Harley-Davidson engine, which was performing really well on my trip so far. At Elly Bay I stopped right on the seashore beside the gentle sand dunes that pop up at this centre point of the peninsula.

Right at the end of the road is Blacksod Point where I stopped at the Blacksod Lighthouse which is unique in Ireland because of its square shape. It was built in 1865 from locally produced granite and also doubled as a weather station until 1957. A sign on the wall of the lighthouse tells us that a D-Day weather forecast was sent from here on 4 June 1944, just before the Allies invaded Normandy. At that time weather forecasting was not the complicated science it is today. Despite Ireland's neutrality during World War II, vital weather information from Ireland was provided to London. The weather forecast from the Blacksod Lighthouse resulted in the invasion being postponed for one day, and ensured that this square building played an important role in history.

The end of the Mullet Peninsula has an interesting short loop that is very much worth riding around. Just past Blacksod Point on the southern part of the loop is a curious group of standing stones on top of a hill at the side of the road. This is one of two such groups of standing stones I saw on this road. However, this is not a Stone Age archaeological site, but rather a circle of stones constructed in 1989 as part of the Mayo Sculpture Trail. This trail, known as *Tír Sáile* in Irish, was one of the largest public arts projects ever undertaken in Ireland. This stone circle is one of fourteen original such sculptures in Mayo and is called 'St Dervla's Twist' after the sixth century saint of the same name. The ruins of her church at Fallmore are reputed to be part of one of the oldest churches in Ireland; she is also thought to be buried in the adjoining cemetery. A little further along the road is a well bearing her name where, according to legend, the waters can cure eye complaints. Not far away in the village of Aghleam, the small Ionad Deirbhile Heritage

St Dervla's Twist

St Dervla's Well

Centre has a stained glass window telling the story of St Dervla. As I sat by the well I enjoyed this peaceful location, thinking that it's no wonder that St Dervla chose this spot for her prayers. Looking towards the south I could still see the back of Slievemore Mountain on Achill Island. To the west the sun was now beginning to set over the Atlantic horizon. I could see the Inishkea Islands where there was once a Norwegian whaling station for a short time between 1908 and 1914.

Back in the town of Belmullet for the evening I went to the Talbot Hotel on main street for a smashing fish and chips dinner and a glass of wine, plus of course free WiFi. I chatted to some local people at the bar who sang the praises of this area. One word that kept being used was 'mighty'. One man told me that Erris Head was 'mighty', while another told me to make sure to visit Doonamo as it too was 'mighty'. On a beautiful evening in Belmullet, I thought they were right.

The next morning my landlady gave me a map and strongly recommended riding to Erris Head at the top of the peninsula. The Mullet Peninsula does not have a circular route so I had to zig-zag across it to see its remote attractions. I aimed first for Ballyglass and had beautiful views over Broadhaven Bay. Once again I stopped at an RNLI Lifeboat Station where a sign tells us that the bay has a reputation for 'treacherous and difficult seas'. In the nineteenth century a number of ships were wrecked here, including one carrying gold which was salvaged and buried by the local people. However, to this day no one knows where the gold was buried and it could still be in the hills around Broadhaven Bay.

At the top of the Mullet Peninsula is Erris Head. The road does not quite go as far as the head itself, but there is a five kilometre Loop Walk which will take you up to the head on foot. This loop is just one of a national network of circular walks that have been developed by Fáilte Ireland. I discovered later that if you kept travelling directly north from here you would pass through the North Pole without touching land again until you reached eastern Siberia.

Erris Head

My next direction was to the western part of the peninsula towards Doonamo Point and Annagh Head. At Doonamo there is another of the Mayo Sculpture Trail sites around a natural blowhole at the edge of a sea-cliff. Two narrow walls form a corridor leading to a circled wall which surrounds the blowhole. Unfortunately, I was not treated to the sight of seawater shooting up from the blowhole. At Annagh Head you will be treated to a great ride through cut bogs and a view towards the small Inishglora Island where, according to legend, the Children of Lir were buried. A few days ago I saw the place near Allihies in County Kerry where they were also reputed to have been buried according to a different legend! Annagh Head is also where you will find the oldest rocks on mainland Ireland, which are 1,753 million years old according to geologists. This location is one of the most remote on the Wild Atlantic Way and is sure to appeal to those who want to 'get away from it all'.

It was time to leave the Mullet Peninsula and move on towards the North Mayo coastline. I travelled around the eastern side of Broadhaven Bay looking back towards where I had been earlier in the morning. The landscape is less desolate for a time as there are a few more trees and houses around. The road runs along the Sruwaddacon Bay, whose unusual name is based on the Irish *Sruth Fada Con*, meaning 'stream of the long hound'. On the road to Benwee Head I was heading towards what for me was one of the most rugged and remote parts of the Wild Atlantic Way. There are many cliffs here, but I was told that to get a real sense of how graceful they look you have to see them from the sea. You can see the cliff that marks Benwee Head, which at 255 metres is higher than the Cliffs of Moher. Another thing that I could see was the first of

Cliffs at the Céide Fields

several heavy showers rolling in from the Atlantic, which I would have to dodge for the rest of the day. With not a single place to take shelter in this most remote of remote locations, I hopped back on the bike and rode east to try to stay ahead of the showers. For kilometre after kilometre I rode inland through endless bogs with one eye on the road and one eye in my mirror watching out for the showers catching up on me.

Just after the tiny village of Belderg I met the coastline again and stopped at the Céide Fields Visitor Centre just in time to beat a heavy shower. *Céide* in Irish means 'flat topped hill', and this is the location of the world's oldest Stone Age field system dating from between five and six thousand years ago. The area has several fields bordered by stone walls, but which for the most part are covered in peat. To get a sense of what this location is all about you have to tour the Visitor Centre where there are plenty of displays of what life was like here dur-

ing the Stone Age and what the extensive layout of the fields looks like. I watched a film about the fields and was fascinated, and envious, to be informed that the climate in Ireland 350 million years ago was tropical! While it poured rain outside I had lunch in the Centre's café and also got chatting to the very helpful OPW guides who shared their expertise with me while I waited for the rain to stop. My first effort at leaving the Céide Fields was thwarted by another shower, and I ran back into the Visitor Centre. This time I got chatting with a French biker who was touring the Wild Atlantic Way on his BMW in the opposite direction to me. We swapped experiences and he whetted my appetite for the rest of the Way. We both agreed that the

Wild Atlantic Way was a unique experience and well worth the effort to get around its many equally unique locations.

Eventually the rain stopped and before leaving the Céide Fields I crossed the road to view the sheer cliff faces that run along the coast. If this area was beside the Cliffs of Moher it would get 'oohs' and 'aahs' all the time. Just after Ballycastle I took a turn left towards Downpatrick Head. This is where you will find the iconic Dún Briste (Broken Fort), which is a sea stack which is separated from the mainland. It is recorded that this separation occurred in the year 1393, though there is also a legend that almost a thousand years earlier St Patrick struck the rock with his crozier when he failed to convert a local chieftain to Christianity. There is a short walk from the end of the road over a couple of fields to cross before you can see Dún Briste. Also located here is another of the Mayo Sculpture Trail sites. This one is called 'Battling Forces', which at first looks like a pile of rocks, but turns out to be a wedge-shaped sculpture with the sharp end pointing out to sea.

The ride from Downpatrick Head to the town of Killala took me around Creevagh Head and on to Lacken Bay. My luck was holding out as I could see rain showers to the left and right of me. At Lacken Bay the tide was out and I could see the fully dried out oval-shaped strand where the Lacken horse races are held each May. Across the bay is Kilcummin where a small French army led by General Jean Humbert landed in August 1798 to help in the rebellion against the British. This also marks the start of the Tour d'Humbert, which traces the route the general and his troops took on their way to the Battle of Killala.

Arriving in Killala the rain finally caught up with me and I took shelter at McDonnell's petrol station where they kindly allowed me to wait out the shower. Overlooking the petrol station is a round tower built at the end of the twelfth century, and when the rain stopped I went around to take a look. One oddity that you can clearly see is that on one side the stone work is bulging out from the almost perfect contours of the tower. This was as a consequence of repairs following a lightning strike in 1840. With nothing else to do but wait for the rain to stop I hummed the tune of the Hal David song 'Rain Drops Keep Falling on my Head', which of course became an *ohrwurm* in my head for the rest of the day.

Leaving Killala I decided to continue on the Tour d'Humbert along the edge of the bay towards Ballina. While I did not see anything related to General Humbert on this road, there are two interesting sites to watch out for. The first is the impressive Moyne Abbey which can be seen clearly from the road. This fifteenth century abbey is relatively intact and is a National Monument in Ireland. Not much further along this road is the more accessible Rosserk Franciscan Friary, which also dates from the fifteenth century. This friary was set up for married men and women who wished to lead a Franciscan lifestyle, but could not join the order given their marital status. Both Moyne Abbey and the Rosserk Friary were burned down in the late sixteenth century by the Governor of Connacht, Richard Bingham. He was responsible for laying waste to many parts of Connacht during rebellions against Queen

Moyne Abbey

Elizabeth I and once ordered that all Spaniards who were shipwrecked on the Irish coast after the failed Armada in 1588 be put to death.

My final port of call in Mayo was the town of Ballina, which is the second largest town in this county. The town lies at the mouth of the River Moy and is regarded by some as the salmon fishing capital of Ireland. The best known memorial to General Humbert is located here on Humbert Street named in his honour. It is a statue featuring the Maid of Erin, and commemorates many people who fought in the cause of Irish freedom. One of the most picturesque parts of Ballina is along the quay on the eastern side of the Moy. There were many boats tied up on the river and the tree-lined western side adds to the almost lake-like peaceful setting.

As I left County Mayo and crossed into County Sligo, I had fond memories of my three days spent touring this most rugged of coast-lines. From Killary Harbour to Ballina Quay there were so many different experiences over the 543 kilometres that my bike and I had travelled. I had seen so much of interest, but also wondered what else I had missed within easy reach of the roads I had been on. As they might say in Mayo, the Wild Atlantic Way is 'mighty'!

6

Sligo and Leitrim –
Short and Shorter

The coastlines around the counties of Sligo and Leitrim are the shortest on the Wild Atlantic Way, but they are not short on interesting places to see and explore. It was early afternoon as I rode into Enniscrone where the beautiful beach makes this one of Sligo's most popular resorts. Many of Sligo's beaches are especially popular for surfers, and at Enniscrone the beach is five kilometres long and is bordered by picturesque sand dunes.

On entering the town I was greeted by the sight of The Black Pig of Muckdubh statue. Muckdubh is a nearby townland where, according to legend, a large black pig is supposed to have been buried after it had run amok in this area before being killed by locals. The Black Pig Festival is held in August each year in honour of this legend. Riding along the beach front I passed by the old Enniscrone Lighthouse which is now part of a block of holiday apartments. Close by on the beach are the old castle-like Cliff Baths, and further along the same road are the Enniscrone Seaweed Baths where you can relax in hot seawater wrapped in seaweed harvested from the Atlantic.

The road around Lenadoon Point at the most northwesterly part of County Sligo is mostly through a flat landscape. At the town of

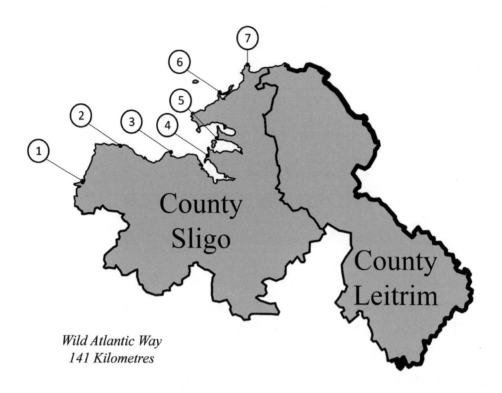

Wild Atlantic Way
141 Kilometres

Wild Atlantic Way – Sligo–Leitrim Discovery Points

1. *Enniscrone Beach*   2. *Easkey Beach*   3. *Aughris & Dunmoran Strand*

4. *Strandhill*   5. *Rosses Point*   6. *Streedagh Point*

7. *Mullaghmore Head*

The Black Pig of Muckdubh

Easkey I stopped to see the ruined O'Dowd Castle near the seafront. This 900-year-old tower house structure dominates the local scenery, and for the most part is still intact. Not far along the road past Easkey is the curious Split Rock which is located in a field at the side of the road opposite Kileenduff National School. Legend has it that the Irish giant, Fionn Mac Cumhaill, split the rock with his sword after an argument with another giant. It is also said that the rock will snap shut if anyone walks through the gap three times. I felt safe because the gap was not wide enough to ride a Harley-Davidson through!

I rode along the narrow roads to Aughris Head where you will find wonderful rock formations of layered limestone exposed at the cliff faces. In the distance I caught my first glimpse of Benbulbin Mountain which dominates the northern part of County Sligo. At Ballysadare I turned left to ride the loop road around the Coolera peninsula to Strandhill. At the centre of the peninsula is Knocknarea hill on top of which there is a large mound of stones. This is reputed to be the location of the grave

Rock formations at Aughris Head

of Queen Maeve, a warrior queen of Connacht in Celtic mythology. She also featured on the Irish pound note before Ireland joined the euro currency. It is considered to be bad luck to remove a stone from the mound, and good luck to deposit one on it.

At the end of the peninsula is the seaside resort of Strandhill where I stopped for a walk along the promenade where a large cannon points out to sea. Despite the poor weather, the village was busy with holiday-makers, several were dressed for hiking around the many walks along the beaches and sand dunes that surround this resort. Just to the north of Strandhill near Sligo airport is Coney Island, which can be reached on foot during low tides. The original name in Irish means 'the island of rabbits', and is one of several possible sources for the name given to Coney Island in New York.

Riding towards Sligo town it was almost impossible for me to keep my eyes on the road because the majestic Benbulbin Mountain kept

The cannon at Strandhill

The wild Atlantic near Strandhill

drawing my eyes northwards. Sligo town is a wonderful mix of old and new buildings. One of the more prominent is the Yeats Memorial Building in Wine Street at the town centre, named in honour of the poet and Nobel Laureate William Butler Yeats. This building hosts the well-known International Yeats Summer School and also features a library and an art gallery. It is a must-stop location for anyone interested in one of Ireland's finest writers. On the same street is Pollexfen House which has a curious turret on the roof where a century ago William Pollexfen, a local ship owner and grandfather to W.B. Yeats, used a telescope to see his ships going in and out of Sligo port.

Leaving Sligo, I rode along the seashore towards Rosses Point. Along the way I stopped at the Radisson Hotel for a coffee and a study of my maps. There were only a few kilometres of Sligo and Leitrim left before I reached County Donegal, and there was still plenty of the

The crowd at Rosses Point

'Waiting on Shore' at Rosses Point

day left to explore some more. Back on the road I arrived at the end of Rosses Point where I stopped to admire the 'Waiting on Shore' bronze sculpture of a girl with her arms stretched out to sea. The sculpture reflects the tradition of people anxiously waiting for loved ones to return from the sea. Right beside the sculpture are the ruins of Elsinore House, which was the home of W.B. Yeats' uncle Henry Middleton. Both W.B. Yeats and his brother Jack spent several summers in Rosses Point, which gave them inspiration for their poetry and painting. From here you can also see in the distance one of Rosses Point's best known attractions, the Metal Man lighthouse, which was built in 1821. It features the Metal Man with an arm outstretched, pointing to the safer waters. He is dressed in the uniform of a British Royal Navy petty officer. The Metal Man is over three and a half metres tall, and weighs seven tonnes. My last stop at Rosses Point was at the main beach which

Grave of W.B. Yeats

runs along Sligo Golf Club. With the tide out, this is a magnificent two kilometre stretch of sand with beautiful views of Knocknarea hill to the south, and of Benbulbin to the north.

Moving on towards north Sligo I stopped at the village of Drumcliff which is best known as the burial place of W.B. Yeats. He died in France in 1939 and it was not until 1948 that he was re-buried in the graveyard of Drumcliff church where his great-grandfather, John Yeats, was rector during the early nineteenth century. The church is built on the location of a monastery founded by St Columcille in the late sixth century. There is also a great example of a Celtic High Cross here, thought to date from the ninth century, which features carvings of stories from the bible. Across the road from the church are the remains of a round tower which dates from the late tenth century. Apparently the top half of the tower was demolished to provide stones for the building of a nearby bridge.

In the small village of Grange I spotted a sign for Streedagh beach and the De Cúellar Trail. Streedagh is a vast, five kilometre-long sandy beach running along sand dunes behind which is a tidal lagoon. As the tide was out, I parked my bike in the middle of the dry lagoon and walked for a while along the beach where I caught my first glimpse of the mountains of south Donegal. Three ships from the Spanish Armada, the *Juliana*, the *La Lavia*, and the *Santa Maria de la Vison*, were wrecked along Streedagh beach in 1588. Many of the surviving sailors were massacred by soldiers from the garrison in Sligo. One survivor was Captain Francisco de Cúellar, who escaped back to Spain and wrote a detailed account of the events in which he constantly refers to the locals as 'savages'. The De Cúellar Trail is named in his memory and there is a monument in the form of the bow of a ship near to the beach at Streedagh.

Round tower at Drumcliff

My next port of call in County Sligo was to the village and harbour of Mullaghmore. The rain had now cleared and I enjoyed the road approaching the village that is dominated on the left side by the late nineteenth century Classiebawn Castle. This was once the summer holiday location for Lord Louis Mountbatten, the last Viceroy of India and a member of the British royal family, who was tragically murdered at Mullaghmore in 1979 at the age of 79. At the side of the road near Classiebawn is an impressive looking modern version of an Ogham stone. Ogham is an old alphabet for the Irish language, typically written on standing stones, with many dating from the fourth century. This one was unveiled in 2006, and carved in Ogham on it are the words in Irish, *Dhá láimh Dé a gcumdach* (the two hands of God around them),

Mullaghmore Harbour

in memory to unbaptised children. At Mullaghmore Harbour there were lots of people about sitting on the many benches that overlook the harbour. This is a popular place for boating and most of the houses seem to be holiday homes. The magnificent eight kilometre-long beach is a surfer's paradise. In 2013, travel website the Lonely Planet named Mullaghmore as one of the 'Best Spots to Catch a Wave' in the world.

My last stop in County Sligo was at the Creevykeel megalithic tomb. This is listed as one of the finest court cairns in Ireland, and is thought to date from the third century B.C. There is an impressive array of stones and you can make out the passageways that were excavated in the 1930s. I walked over the stones and wondered how and why our ancient ancestors created this structure. Today it is just a pile of stones, but in ancient times this was a place where the dead were buried and, despite the passing of over two thousand years, I felt a certain reverence and respect. Leaving the cairn I noticed that there were a lot of white rags and tissues tied to the bushes. Apparently these are symbols of prayer placed by visitors to the cairn.

Soon after Creevykeel I crossed from County Sligo into County Leitrim. I had travelled 141 kilometres around the coast of Sligo, which was the shortest county coastline of my odyssey so far. But at about four kilometres, the Leitrim coast is by far the shortest county coast-line on the Wild Atlantic Way, and indeed of any county in Ireland. I stopped at the county border for a photo opportunity at the 'Wel-come to County Leitrim' sign; I knew it would take just a few minutes to pass through the county. The only village on this stretch of road is Tullaghan, where there is a High Cross on a mound at the centre of the village. This tenth century cross is distinctive in that it leans to one

Creevykeel megalithic tomb

side. This is not its original location. It is thought that it was moved to Tullaghan to protect it from coastal erosion and that it was once part of an ancient monastery.

So far it had been a long day since leaving Belmullet early in the morning, and by now it was late afternoon. Having dodged rain showers for most of the day I decided to keep going on into the evening as there were many hours of daylight left. The short and shorter coastal roads of Counties Sligo and Leitrim may be the quickest part of the Wild Atlantic Way, but I had enjoyed every moment of the ride from Enniscrone in west Sligo to Tullaghan in Leitrim.

Welcome to County Leitrim

7

DONEGAL – WILD AND REMOTE

The county of Donegal is the last on my exploration of the Wild Atlantic Way, and it is with some excitement that my bike and I roared across the border from County Leitrim in the early evening. I had only paid two short visits before to the land once known as Tyrconnell. With a very long coastline and 36 Discovery Points to check out, I knew I would be in for a treat riding around this wild and sometimes remote corner of Ireland.

The county is named after the town of Donegal, *Dún na nGall*, which means 'fort of the foreigners'. This name was given when the Vikings invaded in the eighth century and built a garrison in what is now Donegal town. I felt a bit like a foreigner coming to a strange land, but the people of Donegal have a great welcome for all visitors to their shores.

Bundoran, known as Ireland's premier seaside resort, was my first stop in Donegal. In the early evening it was bustling with tourists, many out walking on the promenade that circles the town. Perched high over the rocky shore is one of Bundoran's main attractions, Water World, which is an indoor aqua adventure centre. Beside it is a small park and I stopped for a brief look at a sculpture consisting of a standing stone surrounded by an arch, known as the Rock of the Birds. The promenade continues around Bundoran Golf Club, but it is accessible only

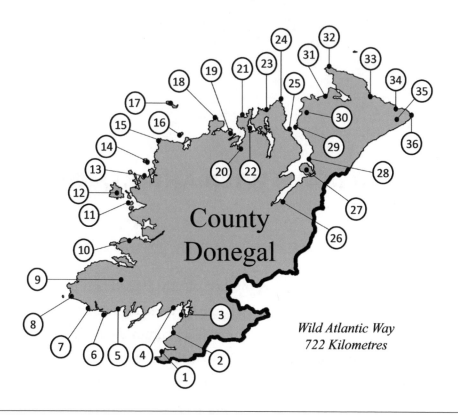

Wild Atlantic Way – Donegal Discovery Points

1. Tullan Strand	2. Rossnowlagh Beach	3. Murvagh Beach
4. Mountcharles Pier	5. Fintragh Bay	6. Muckros Head
7. Slieve League	8. Malin Beg	9. Glengesh Pass
10. Narin-Portnoo Strand	11. Inishfree	12. Arranmore
13. Carrickfinn Beach	14. Gola Island	15. Bloody Foreland
16. Inishbofin	17. Tory Island	18. Horn Head
19. Marble Hill	20. Doe Castle	21. Rosguill Peninsula
22. Island Roy	23. Ballyhiernan Bay	24. Fanad Head
25. Ballymastocker Strand	26. Manorcunningham	27. Inch Island
28. Lisfannon Beach	29. Dunree Head	30. Mamore Gap
31. Pollan Bay	32. Malin Head	33. Culdaff Beach
34. Kinnagoe Bay	35. Magilligan Point	36. Inishowen Head

The author on Abbey Mill Bridge, possibly the oldest bridge in Ireland

by foot. I rode around to the start of Tullan Strand, the first of many beautiful beaches that stretch around the coast of Donegal.

Ballyshannon is just a few kilometres from Bundoran and claims to be the oldest town in Ireland. I parked the bike outside Fin Mc-Cool's pub and walked the short distance to see the bronze statue of rock musician Rory Gallagher, who was born in Ballyshannon in 1948. This is a magnificent monument to one of Ireland's greatest rockers and depicts him in full flow with his guitar. Songs such as 'Follow Me' and 'Tattoo'd Lady' started to play in my head. Back at my bike a man calling himself 'The Fiddler' introduced

Statue of Rory Gallagher in Ballyshannon

himself to me as one of the three men who placed the statue into its position.

Ballyshannon is also the birthplace of William Allingham, the 'Bard of Ballyshannon', who was best known for his poem 'The Faeries'. On the outskirts of the town on the road to Rossnowlagh are the remains of Abbey Assaroe and Catsby Cave, where you can see a rock in this secluded and peaceful place where Mass was celebrated in secret during Penal Times in the eighteenth century. Also of interest here is what is thought to be Ireland's oldest bridge. The Abbey Mill Bridge was probably built by the Cistercian monks in the twelfth century.

Before arriving in Donegal town I visited two more beaches at Rossnowlagh and Murvagh. These two beaches are joined together and run continuously for about 10 kilometres. The road takes you past extensive dunes leading to Murvagh Forest which is a designated Special Area of Conservation. This is possibly the most remote beach I have ever been to, and if you are looking for unspoilt sand dunes this is the place to go.

In Donegal town I first stopped at the Discover Ireland tourist office beside the River Eske where the fantastic staff helped me with selecting information on touring Donegal's coast line. Close by the town centre is the restored Donegal Castle. Though closed for the evening I could get a sense of its magnificence from the road outside. It was first built in 1474 by the O'Donnell chieftains and was once referred to in 1566 by the Lord Deputy for Ireland, Sir Henry Sidney, as the 'largest and strongest fortress in all Ireland'.

As the evening started to close in I set out for Killybegs as my last stop for the day. On the way I took a quick detour down to Mountcharles Pier where I could see across Donegal Bay to the beach at Murvagh where I had been earlier. The road runs right along the seashore here and riding along it was a very pleasant way to spend a summer's evening. I finally arrived in Killybegs and found a room for the night at the comfortable Seawinds B&B in the town centre where I was made very welcome by the owner Patricia. I had dinner in the Tara Hotel overlooking the harbour where the huge fishing trawlers towered over the quayside. This is one of Ireland's biggest fishing ports based in a natural deep water harbour. More than 100,000 tonnes of fish are landed here annually which accounts for about 45 per cent of the total fish landed by Irish vessels in Ireland. Even here in the harbour, locals were fishing with rods from the pier and seemed to be able to catch a fish every time they reeled in their fishing lines. Nearby is a poignant reminder of the ultimate price some fishermen pay on a granite stone showing over 100 names of those who 'gave their lives to the sea'.

The next morning I was treated to a wonderful full Irish breakfast cooked by Patricia. By now I was becoming a connoisseur of this big breakfast after having so many rashers, sausages, eggs and black

Killybegs Harbour

pudding on this trip. I shared a table with two Canadians from Toronto who were touring Scotland and Ireland on their Harley-Davidson Road King. We looked like a mini-Hell's Angels gang in our leathers and Harley-Davidson t-shirts at breakfast. They were very enthusiastic about the Wild Atlantic Way which they were part completing in the opposite direction to me. We shared travel experiences and our love of big motorcycles, and gave each other tips on sights to see. I sensed not only the usual biker camaraderie, but also a shared passion for riding the Wild Atlantic Way. Before leaving, Patricia gave me a hand-drawn map of the sights to see in this part of southwest Donegal, so I set off in the early morning anticipating the many delights that awaited.

I did not have long to wait before stopping at the beautiful Fintragh strand where only a low sand dune separates the sea from a GAA football field. At Muckros Head I stopped briefly to admire the layered and overhanging rocks which are popular with climbers. But the most spectacular rocks in this region are a little bit further west at the Slieve League cliffs. The twisty road from the village of Teelin was already busy with buses and camper vans all going in one direction towards the cliffs. I rode right up to the second car park which overlooks the cliffs and parked the bike in the best spot I could get for some biker-themed photographs of the cliffs. Despite the mist I was blown away by the size and majesty of these stunning cliffs. At almost 600 metres they are twice as high as the Cliffs of Moher and are among the highest and finest marine cliffs in Europe. There are some spectacular trails for walkers, including the legendary One Man's Pass, which is a narrow path that is regarded as one of the most outstanding walks to be found in Ireland. I walked up the path from the car park to get a better view of the cliffs, but no matter where you stand here you are surrounded by stunning scenery. This was definitely one of the highlights of my trip so far.

Riding back through Teelin I then made my way around Slieve League to see both Malin More and Malin Beg. Here I was at the most

Slieve League cliffs

western part of County Donegal and, in complete contrast to the Slieve League cliffs, there was not a soul to be seen at the Silver Strand at the end of the road in Malin Beg. This is a beautiful strand surrounded on three sides by high banks of land that show signs of erosion caused by the wild Atlantic. There are 160 steps down to the beach, but only sheep were venturing down this early in the morning. In the distance I could see a tower and decided to ride over to get a closer look. I didn't anticipate the dreadful state of the lane leading up to it, but my Harley-Davidson was up to the challenge. The tower was built in 1806 as a watchtower during the Napoleonic Wars to look out for an invasion from the French that never materialised. The tower overlooks a small

The Silver Strand at Malin Beg

island with the curious name of Rathlin O'Birne. Here was based Ireland's first nuclear powered lighthouse from 1974 to 1987, though it is now powered by solar energy.

I reached the historic village of Glencolmcille in the mid-morning and stopped at the Folk Village. This tourist attraction is built in the form of a village of small thatched cottages which are exact replicas of those lived in by local people in the eighteenth to twentieth centuries. The folk village was set up by local priest Fr James McDyer in 1967 in an effort to create badly needed employment for people of the area. It offers a glimpse into the daily lives of the people of Donegal as it was during the past few centuries, and is well worth a visit. Glencolmcille is of course named after St Colmcille (also known as St Columba) who, along with St Patrick and St Brigid, is one of the three patron saints of

Ireland. The scenery here is fantastic, especially from the northern side of the glen where I rode around to see St Columcille's Chapel and Well. He was born in northern Donegal, but it is thought that he also lived here for two years before he set off to convert Scotland to Christianity in the year 563.

After Glencolmcille I had to take the road inland as there is no coastal road for much of this part of Donegal. The road over the hills and mountains reminded me a lot of north Mayo as there is plenty of peat bogs dominating the landscape. There is a real treat at Glengesh Pass where the road suddenly opens up to the almost alpine view of the valley that leads to the heritage town of Ardara. The hairpin bends, steep roads and high hills make this a unique ride in Ireland. At Ardara it was time for a break and I stopped at the Heritage Centre where I

Glencolmcille Folk Village

Glengesh Pass

had a coffee outside in the sun. The Heritage Centre was set up in 1992 to showcase the local Donegal tweed industry, and it is also home to the local tourist office. Ardara has been dubbed the 'Festival Capital of Donegal' and includes the curiously named 'Cup of Tae' festival which features workshops and a school of music for traditional musicians. Close to the Heritage Centre was a sign and map which displayed the Duquesta Santa Anna Drive, which is named after yet another Spanish Armada ship that was wrecked off the Atlantic coast at Rosbeg, 13 kilometres from Ardara. The *Duquesta Santa Anna* had 357 men on board, many of whom survived but were later drowned when another Spanish ship, called the *La Girona*, sank off the coast of County Antrim with the loss of over 1,000 lives. So I set off around this drive which is about 20 kilometres long and circles around several scenic small lakes and narrow roads. This route includes the Bonny Glen Lough Drive, which is named after a small lake and woods of the same name. Along the way is Narin-Portnoo Strand, where when the tide is out you can walk across to Inishkeel Island where there are wonderful standing stones with crosses carved on the sides, as well as the ruins of two twelfth century churches.

At the start of the region known as The Rosses I entered the town of Dungloe, which is the largest town in the Donegal Gaeltacht, and also home to the famous Mary from Dungloe International Festival. You don't have to be called 'Mary' to be a contestant, but if you win you will be crowned 'Mary of Dungloe' for a year. The festival takes place in August each year and brings thousands of tourists to the region. The

Ardara

The Arranmore Ferry in Burtonport

Rosses, which includes the islands of Inishfree and Arranmore, is an area of outstanding natural beauty. The area has over 120 small lakes dotted around the rocky landscape, around which the Wild Atlantic Way winds its route around some excellent views of the many islands associated with The Rosses.

Signs in Irish

From Dungloe I travelled the scenic coastal route to Burtonport where I stopped at the small harbour. Here you can get a ferry out to Arranmore, which is the second largest island off the Irish coast. You can see several other islands from the harbour, including Inishfree, which was once home to a group of free thinkers, known as the Atlantis Foundation, who formed a community on the island in 1974. The community was known locally as

'The Screamers' due to their practice of screaming loudly as a form of therapy. A sudden heavy shower forced me to seek shelter and I made my way up the street to a restaurant with a giant red lobster attached to the outside wall. This Kelly family-run pub and restaurant is called the Lobster Pot where I had a delicious lunch of seafood chowder and brown bread.

Leaving Burtonport I continued to circle around The Rosses. This is a Gaeltacht region where signs in Irish only can make finding your way around a bit difficult for the non-Irish speaker. I travelled through the small village of Kincasslagh, best known as the home where singer Daniel O'Donnell grew up, and on to yet another one of Donegal's finest beaches at Carrickfinn which runs alongside Donegal Airport. The winding road around The Rosses is completed at the village of Crolly, which gave its name to the world famous Crolly Dolls. Looking inland there are wonderful views of Mount Errigal, which at 571 metres is the highest mountain in Donegal. It is one of a chain of mountains known as the 'Seven Sisters' and is listed as Ireland's Most Iconic Mountain by the *Walking and Hiking Ireland* magazine.

At Bunbeg there is a small picturesque harbour overlooking Gweedore Bay, and from here ferry boats travel to the islands of Gola and Tory. Bunbeg is part of the region called Gweedore, which is one of the most densely populated rural areas in Europe. The huge number of bungalows scattered around the landscape is testament to this, but it still must be a beautiful place to live in. At the extreme northwest of Gweedore is Bloody Foreland. Despite its gory sounding name, Bloody Foreland gets its name from the way the setting sun shines on the red granite sea cliffs. From here you can also see Tory Island which is 14.5 kilometres from the mainland. A little further along this road at Meenlaragh there is a splendid view of Inishbofin Island, and an almost perfectly formed moon-shaped beach that protects Ballyness Bay, which is an important water fowl habitat. Riding around this bay I passed through Gortahork, where outside the local school you will see

Bunbeg Harbour

an interesting statue of a man with a scythe. The flat-topped Muckish Mountain dominates the landscape in this area, and it too is one of the 'Seven Sisters' mountains.

By now it was getting late and I decided that it was time to settle down for the evening. I stopped in the town of Dunfanaghy, but quickly found that all accommodation in the town was booked out. One very kind landlady helped me get a bed for the night by calling the Forest Lodge B&B just outside Dunfanaghy where I was well looked after by Jean. She recommended riding up to the top of the nearby Horn Head to see the sun setting, so off I set for my final ride of the day on what was once called 'the finest headland in Ireland' by Robert Lloyd Praeger in his 1937 book *The Way That I Went*. I rode all the way up to the end of the road near a World War II lookout tower where I met a Scottish couple who were having the sights pointed out to them by a local man. He pointed out Tory Island to the west, and the Rosguill peninsula to the east over Sheephaven Bay. He told us about the 180 metre cliffs on the eastern side of the head, and where best to view them from. Below us was the small Crockshee hill that stands out from the bog and heather-covered landscape. With the evening starting to get darker, I rode around the eastern side of Horn Head and stopped on a hill overlooking Dunfanaghy where I watched the silhouettes of the hills and mountains in the absolute quiet of this peaceful location. For dinner I stopped at the Starfish Café on the main street in Dunfanaghy, where I enjoyed a delicious meal of sea bass. I ended the day with a nice pint in Patsy Dan's Bar where I looked back over my photos of the day and examined my maps as I looked forward to travelling around the remainder of Donegal on what would be my last day on the Wild Atlantic Way.

Next morning I set out on the last, but very long, part of my journey. At the village of Portnablaghy I stopped for one final look back at

Muckish Mountain overlooking Ballyness Bay

Horn Head and then took the short detour from the main road down to Marble Hill beach which is located just below the Shandon Hotel and Marble Hill holiday park. This beach looks out on to the calm waters of Sheephaven Bay and across to the Rosguill peninsula. It was a peaceful location this early in the morning, with not a soul out on the beach. Back on the main road I noticed a sign to the left for the Ards Friary, but decided to give it a miss. A few hundred metres further along the road there was another sign, which I also passed. But on seeing a third sign for the friary I just had to investigate. The friary is down along a narrow road that runs beside the Ards Forest Park. The Ards Friary is a retreat and conference centre formerly run by the Capuchin Franciscans, and it is set in a location where you can take time out from the stress-filled and hectic lives we lead. I took a short walk around some of the grounds and enjoyed the ride through the woods leading back to the main road.

Statue of St Francis of Assisi at Ards Friary

Doe Castle

Riding towards the village of Creeslough I saw some of the ruins at the side of the road of a large railway viaduct, once part of the Lough Swilly Railway which was closed in 1953. This was also the scene of what was known as the Owencarrow Viaduct Disaster, when 190 kilometre per hour winds derailed a passenger train from the viaduct in 1925. Four people were killed in what was the Lough Swilly Railway's worst ever accident. Cresslough is in a beautiful setting near the foot of Muckish Mountain, and was once the home of Bridie Gallagher who was born and reared here. Bridie is often thought of as one of Ireland's first international pop stars, and is more affectionately known as 'The Girl from Donegal'.

Just past Creeslough is the picturesque Doe Castle, which is located at the southern end of Sheephaven Bay. It was built in the early sixteenth century by the McSweeney family who were chiefs in this area. The castle changed hands many times during English/Irish conflict over the subsequent centuries. It was the location where Irish general Owen Roe O'Neill, a member of the great earls of Tyrone O'Neill family, landed in 1642. He was also a soldier who famously led the Irish army to victory over the English in 1646 at the Battle of Benburb. Doe Castle is closed to visitors, but it is possible to walk right up to the walls. It is a four-storey tower house surrounded by a wall and moat. The white walls of the tower contrast sharply with the grey walls that surround the castle. Riding around to the eastern side of Sheephaven Bay the castle is visible for many kilometres and it is not difficult to see why the McSweeneys chose this location to build a castle.

On top of the Rossguill Peninsula

I was now on my way northwards to the Rosguill peninsula. There is a well-established Atlantic Drive around this short peninsula which has the village of Downings as its main centre. At the top of the peninsula there are beautiful views westwards towards Horn Head, where the cliffs look majestic in the distance. While there are a lot of holiday makers about, there is a quiet calm about the place with some beaches on the northern side of the peninsula totally deserted. The eastern side of the peninsula runs along Mulroy Bay where the Atlantic drive ends near Island Roy. This small island, which can be reached by a narrow causeway, is not named after a person called 'Roy'. Instead it gets its name from the Irish name for *Oilean Ruaidh*, which means 'Red Island', so-named because of the rusty red coloured vegetation in winter time.

The Rosguill and Fanad peninsulas are now connected by the Harry Blaney Bridge which is named after a local politician. Given its remote location it has been dubbed 'the bridge to nowhere', but it is a brilliant piece of engineering that cuts over an hour from the drive around the rest of Mulroy Bay and Broad Water to the other side. I continued on towards Fanad Head at the very end of the peninsula. Before reaching the head I stopped at the freshwater Lough Kindrum where a sign tells you what the best flies – with wonderful names like 'Golden Olive Bumble' and 'Butcher' – are to use for fishing. At the water's edge is a Celtic cross monument erected in 1960 to 'three Fanad patriots' – Neil Shiels, Michael Heraghty, and Michael McElwee – who 'ended the tyranny of landlordism' in 1878. They did this by taking part in the murder of the third Earl of Leitrim, William Sydney Clements, who was notorious in Irish history for poor treatment of tenants.

At Fanad Head, the white late nineteenth century lighthouse stands proud at the tip of the Fanad peninsula. Curiously, there is a World War II lookout tower very close by and I wondered why the lookouts could not have used the lighthouse instead. There is also a ruined coast guard station as this was a strategic location during World War I when

Fanad Lighthouse

Ireland was still part of the United Kingdom. Lough Swilly lies to the eastern side of the Fanad peninsula and it was the main Atlantic base for the Allied fleet during the war. Looking across Lough Swilly you can see Dunaff Head on the Inishowen peninsula, but there is no bridge between the two peninsulas so it is a 110 kilometre ride down and up both sides of the lough. At the village of Portsalon I stopped at the small harbour to take in the view across Ballymastocker Strand, which must be one of the finest golden strands in the world. The strand is about three kilometres long and is best viewed from hills above the southern side of the beach. This beach was where a British naval warship, the *Saldanha*, tragically met its end in a storm during the Napoleonic Wars in 1811. It was captained by 29-year-old William Pakenham, a brother-in-law to the Duke of Wellington who was victor over Napoleon at the Battle of Waterloo. The entire ship's company of over 250 sailors died in the

Ballymastocker Strand

tragedy, including Pakenham himself who perished on Ballymastocker Strand despite efforts by locals to revive him with *poitín*.

From Portsalon, through Rathmullan, and on to Rathmelton the road hugs the coastline. At Rathmullan there is a ferry service to Buncrana on the Inishowen peninsula, but I decided to keep going all the way around Lough Swilly. Just south of Portsalon you can see the first of seven coastal forts, this one called Knockalla, which dot the shores of Lough Swilly. Another one of these forts overlooks the harbour in Rathmullan which is now part of the Flight of the Earls Heritage Centre. It was from this location in 1607 that the Earl of Tír Eóghain (Tyrone), Hugh Ó Neill, and the Earl of Tír Chonaill (present day Donegal), Rory Ó Donnell, left Ireland never to return. This event is regarded as a defining moment in Irish history as it marked the ending of the ancient Gaelic order in Ireland. On the other side of the harbour car park is a magnificent bronze sculpture by John Behan depicting the moment the earls embarked on their ship with about 100 followers. Seven months later they arrived in Rome and were received by Pope Paul V.

The heritage town of Rathmelton is a quiet, beautiful town that sits at the mouth of the river Leannan. Along the river's edge are some old warehouses which were built in the early to mid-nineteenth century. In the days of sail this was a busy port with ships trading regularly between Rathmelton, New York and Jamaica, carrying linen and foodstuffs such as salted fish and dairy products. This area was home to the O'Donnell clan who were rulers of Donegal from the twelfth century until the Flight of the Earls in 1607. And 176 years later another man left this location to go to Pennsylvania in America in 1783. He was James Buchanan Sr who was born in Rathmelton. His eldest son, also called James, became the fifteenth President of the United States in 1857, and was the predecessor to Abraham Lincoln. Another one of Rathmelton's famous sons is Samuel Gamble Bayne who emigrated from here to America in the late 1860s. He became a billionaire after making his fortune in gold and oil and he was a founder of

River Leannan in Rathmelton

the Seaboard National Bank in 1883, which ultimately became Chase Manhattan Bank (now JP Morgan Chase). Two hundred years earlier another Rathmelton native, Francis Makemie, left Donegal as a missionary in 1683 for Virginia where he is considered to be the founder of the Presbyterian Church in America. These emigrants are a testament to the people of Rathmelton and the region's influence on the other side of the Atlantic.

Right at the southern tip of Lough Swilly is Letterkenny, which is the largest town in County Donegal. Unfortunately, as I approached the town the skies darkened quickly and I had to seek refuge from a thunderstorm in the Mount Errigal Hotel, but as it was time for lunch I did not mind too much. I looked up the weather online and it seemed that there would be quite a lot of shower activity for the rest of the day. I still had the Inishowen peninsula to ride, which would be a distance of around 160 kilometres. After lots of hot tea, I kitted myself out in rain gear and set off towards Malin Head, the northern most point in Ireland.

I stopped briefly at Manorcunningham for a view back towards Letterkenny and continued on in light rain until I reached the village of Burt. Here I visited the stone fort built on top of a hill called *Grianán of Aileach* ('Stone Palace of the Sun'), from which there is a magnificent view of the surrounding countryside. It is thought that the fort was built around the time of the birth of Christ with walls that are 4.5 metres thick in places. Inside there are three terraced walkways, and it is easy to get right to the top. During the autumn equinox the sun shines directly through the entrance and cuts a path of light right across the centre of the fort. From the top I looked down at Lough Swilly and the

Grianán of Aileach

nearby Inch Island, which is a wildfowl reserve. The fort is quite big, with an internal diameter of just over 23 metres and walls five metres high. It must have taken quite an effort to bring this much stone to the top of a hill, and walking around the walls I could only admire the handiwork of our ancestors from over 2,000 years ago.

Just past Burt is the village of Bridgend which marks the start of the Inishowen 100. This is a driving route that is signposted around the largest peninsula in Ireland which is about 100 miles (160 kilometres) long. The name Inishowen comes from the Irish *Inis Eoghain*, which means 'Island of Eoghan', and it thought to be named after the fifth century prince Eoghan mac Néill. He was the son of a High King of Ireland called Niall of the Nine Hostages. He was reputedly baptised by St Patrick and is buried in Iskaheen close to the end of the Wild Atlantic Way. My first name in Irish is *Eoghan* and I felt somewhat at home in Inishowen.

Riding up the western side of the Inishowen peninsula I stopped at the village of Fahan where a small modern marina is located beside the remains of an old wooden pier. The poet and hymn writer Cecil Frances Alexander, who was married to the Bishop of Derry and wrote two of the most famous Christian hymns, 'Once in Royal David's City' and 'All Things Bright and Beautiful', lived here in the late 1850s. Nearby is Liscannon beach which looks out over Lough Swilly to Rathmullan on the other side. Just five kilometres north of Fahan is Inishowen's largest and busiest town, Buncrana. The centre of the town circles around narrow one way streets. I took a left turn in the town centre down to the shore where the ruins of Cahir O'Doherty's Keep and Buncrana Castle are located. The castle lies on the river Crana, from which Buncrana gets its name, and was built in the early eighteenth century. It is accessible across a narrow picturesque arched bridge, and it was here that Theobald Wolfe Tone was held after he was arrested nearby on 3 November 1798 during the failed United Irishmen Rebellion. He was taken from here to jail in Dublin where he was tried for treason on 8

November, convicted, and sentenced to death, though he cheated the hangman by slitting his own throat. Despite this he is revered in Irish history to this day.

Just outside Buncrana is the former British fort called Ned's Point, which was built during the Napoleonic Wars in 1812. I had not yet been inside any of the seven forts that dot Lough Swilly, but I was able to fix that further up the coast at Fort Dunree which is located at Dunree Head. The fort is positioned in a dramatic location on top of a rocky outcrop. It is now a museum and is well worth the time it takes to tour around the inside of the sometimes cramped conditions that the fort's inhabitants had to work in. The museum features a fascinating collection of military artefacts and guns, some of which are still fired on occasion. There are many derelict huts which once housed the soldiers who

Fort Dunree

staffed the fort. It was here that the final ceremony of the handing over of three treaty ports by the British to the Irish took place on 3 October 1938, just before the start of World War II. On the long straight road up the nearby Urris Hills, there is a wonderful view back towards Dunree Head and to the Fanad Peninsula on the other side of Lough Swilly.

This part of Donegal is much less populated than elsewhere in the county. Here, the long narrow roads reach a wonderful zenith at Mamore Gap in an area known as Amazing Grace Country. The writer of the words for the famous hymn 'Amazing Grace' was Englishman John Newton. Prior to becoming a clergyman he was a slave trader whose ship was saved in 1748 from certain sinking in a violent storm by taking shelter in Lough Swilly. Local people here helped Newton and his colleagues, and it is thought that this experience later inspired him to write the famous words in which he as a 'wretch' who was 'lost' and was 'found' by a merciful God. Though Newton only spent a short while in Donegal it is a fascinating connection between this beautiful land and the writer of one of the world's best-known hymns.

I parked at the top of the Mamore Gap, which is 260 metres above sea level, to take in the views north out to the Atlantic and south to Inishowen. It is a popular location for tourists to visit and explore the nearby hills. Just past the top of the Gap is St Eigne's Well which also features statues of Our Lady. From here there is an excellent view towards the prominent hill on Dunaff Head. The road down from Mamore Gap was very winding, but it was good fun to ride. Two really nice beaches to see here are at Tullagh Bay and Pollan Bay, both of which were deserted.

By now I was riding across the northern coastline of the Inishowen Peninsula. At Clonmany I stopped to admire the remains of St Columba's church which was built in 1772. The church was closed in the 1920s and had been dedicated to St Columba. According to local legend, a stone in the adjoining graveyard features the tracks of his knees and any water that lodges in the tracks is said to have curative

Tullagh Bay

powers. Coming into the town of Carndonagh I stopped to see the seventh century Donagh Cross, which is thought to be one of the earliest High Crosses in Ireland. Cardonagh is centred on a beautiful square called 'The Diamond', and the town is dominated by the magnificent Church of the Sacred Heart. Each brick made for this church, built in 1945 in a neo-Romanesque style, was hand-carved and laid by master stonemasons from all over Ireland. Leading into the village of Malin I crossed over the ten arch bridge, reputedly the second oldest stone bridge in Ireland, which spans this part of Trabreaga Bay. From here I rode along the Lagg Road towards Malin Head past some of the highest sand dunes in Europe.

The most northerly point in Ireland is located at Banba's Crown on Malin Head. Depending on the road you take, this most northerly point is between 600 and 700 kilometres from Ireland's most south-westerly point at Mizen Head. The trip from Malin to Mizen is a popular challenge, especially for cyclists, which charities undertake to raise money. I had arrived here ten days after setting out from Dublin and it was definitely worth the ride to come to this place of scenic beauty and geographic significance. It was a surprise to me that a caravan selling freshly made coffee was located here, so I bought myself an espresso and sat down on the rocks to look out on the Atlantic knowing that there was nowhere in Ireland, apart from a few island rocks, further north than here. I had come a long way and I was on a high feeling like I had climbed a mountain to get here.

Malin Head has been an important communications location for over 200 years. The British Army built a tower here in 1805 during the Napoleonic Wars which still stands. A signal station was also built beside the tower, and there are concrete huts dating from World War II that were used as lookout posts. During the war the Irish government allowed the British to use two wireless direction-finding stations at Malin. From here you can also see the small island of Inishtrahull, which is about 10 kilometres off shore. Beside it are several small islands called the Tor Rocks. One of these is called Tor Beg and this is the actual most northerly point in Ireland. Inishtrahull Island features a lighthouse that was built in 1958, replacing an older lighthouse that dated back

Malin Head lookout tower

to 1812. The Gneiss rocks on the island are older than the rocks at An-nagh Head in County Mayo that I saw a few days earlier, and at over 1.7 billion years the oldest rocks anywhere in Ireland. It is with a little bit of sadness that I left Malin Head in the early evening as for the first time I was heading in the direction towards home, but there was still the last part of the Wild Atlantic Way to ride.

My next destination was Inishowen Head on the northeastern side of the peninsula. I took the winding roads along the coastline through the village of Culdaff where I stopped to view the fine golden sandy beach of the same name. Further along the coast is Kinnagoe Bay where the high dunes make for a great backdrop along the beach. It was here that another of the Spanish Armada ships, the *Trinidad Valencera*, ran aground in 1588. At about 1,000 tonnes it was one of the largest ships in the Armada. The crew survived the shipwreck only to be massacred by local soldiers. The wreck of the ship was discovered by the City of Derry Sub-Aqua Club in 1971, and several of its cannons are now on view in the Ulster Museum in Belfast.

One of the best views in this part of Donegal is at the Magilligan Point View which is on the road to Moville. From here I got my first glimpse of County Derry on the other side of Lough Foyle, and it is a splendid ride down to the town of Moville and its small harbour. Overlooking the harbour is a neat row of Victorian houses with lovely bay windows, which forms part of Montgomery Terrace. This terrace was built in 1884 by Sir Robert Montgomery who was born in Moville in 1809. He later worked as a colonial administrator in India, and it was his grandson Bernard who became Field Marshall Montgomery of Alamein.

Further along the coast is the fishing port of Greencastle. The town is named after a castle which is now in ruins. Though it is almost cov-ered in green ivy, it is thought that the name comes from the green stone with which the castle was built in 1305. Richard de Burgo, who was known as the Red Earl of Ulster, established the castle as a base

Ruined castle in Greencastle

for Norman power in Donegal. It was badly damaged in 1555 when the O'Doherty and O'Donnell chiefs fought a war in which cannons were used to reduce the castle to ruin. It is worth stopping to take a look at the remains of the towers and walls that are still standing after 700 years. Close to the castle is the National Fisheries College where students are trained in sea fishing, fish farming, and seafood processing. Greencastle is also home to the Inishowen Maritime Museum & Planetarium which is located in the old coastguard station overlooking the harbour. It features many maritime artefacts and is a great way to spend an hour learning about the rich sea heritage of the Inishowen Peninsula.

Back on the road again I rode up to the last Discovery Point of the Wild Atlantic Way at Inishowen Head. Here the Shroove Lighthouse,

Shroove Lighthouse

which was built in 1837, overlooks the beautiful and compact Shroove beach. On a fine day the west coast of Scotland can be seen from here, and there are several more great views on the coastal walk around the Inishowen Head Walk which reaches the scenic Shoulder of Crocknasmug at its highest point. It was time to turn south for the final time and I went back towards Greencastle via the narrow high road that provides great views over Lough Foyle. I stopped at a holy well dedicated to St Brigid, a small stone cross sits on top of the well. St Brigid lived in the time of St Patrick, and the famous Brigid's Cross, which is made from rushes, is named after her. She is reputedly buried beside St Patrick in County Down.

Just past Moville, I made my final stop on the Wild Atlantic Way at a small pier. It was late evening and I took one last look at the still waters of Lough Foyle. I had travelled 722 kilometres around the coast of Donegal over three days. I stood beside my Harley-Davidson and felt in my heart that together we had completed a fantastic journey. I was already thinking of how to write up my account which I would start the next day. I set out for the City of Derry and the long road to Dublin wishing I could instead take the long way home by retracing my route around the Wild Atlantic Way. But my motorcycle odyssey had come to an end.

The odyssey ends at Lough Foyle

Saying farewell to the Wild Atlantic Way
(photo by Kathleen Kelleher)

Sources

360 Ireland (www.360eire.com)

Achill Tourism (www.achilltourism.com)

Allihies Copper Mine Museum (www.acmm.ie)

Augusteijn, J. (2010). *Patrick Pearse: The Making of a Revolutionary*. Palgrave MacMillan.

Beara Tourism (www.bearatourism.com)

Baltimore & the Isles (www.baltimore.ie)

Clare County Library (www.clarelibrary.ie)

Coast Guards of Yesteryear (www.coastguardsofyesteryear.org)

Commissioners of Irish Lights (www.commissionersofirishlights.com)

Connemara National Park (www.connemaranationalpark.ie)

Connemara Tourism (www.connemara.ie)

de Cúellar, Francisco. Captain Cuellar's Adventures in Connacht and Ulster. Available at: http://www.ucc.ie/celt/online/T108200/text002.html

Destination Westport (www.destinationwestport.com)

Discover Ireland (www.discoverireland.ie)

Donegal Islands (www.donegalislands.com)

Fáilte Ireland (www.failteireland.ie)

Fleming, B. (2009). *The Vatican Pimpernel: The Wartime Exploits of Monsignor Hugh O'Flaherty.* The Collins Press.

Foynes Flying Boat Museum (www.flyingboatmuseum.com)

Galway History (www.galwayhistory.info)

Galway Ireland Tourism (www.galwaytourism.ie)

Geograph Ireland (www.geograph.ie)

GeoNeed (www.geoneed.org)

Go Strandhill (gostrandhill.com)

Heaney, S. (2001). *The Spirit Level.* Faber & Faber.

Heritage Ireland (www.heritageireland.ie)

Hidden Ireland (www.hiddenireland.com)

Holiday **Tralee (www.holidaytralee.com)**

Inishowen Heritage (www.inishowenheritage.ie)

Ingenious Ireland (www.ingeniousirelandonline.ie)

Inishowen Maritime Museum & Planetarium (www.inishowenmaritime.com)

Ireland View (www.irelandview.com)

Irish Antiquities (irishantiquities.bravehost.com)

Irish Aviation Authority (www.iaa.ie)

Joyce, P.W., Sullivan, A.M., Nunan, P.D. (1900). *Atlas and Cyclopedia of Ireland.* New York: Murphy & McCarthy

Killybegs Information Centre (www.killybegs.ie)

Kinvara Online (www.kinvara.com)

Kylemore Abbey & Victorian Walled Garden (www.kylemoreabbeytourism.ie)

Lalor, B. (2003). *The Encylopedia of Ireland.* Gill & Macmillan.

Landed Estates Database, NUI Galway (landedestates.nuigalway.ie)

Legend Quest (www.legendquest.ie)

Sources

Leitrim Tourism (www.leitrimtourism.com)

Lochnan, K. (2011) "Corcomroe Abbey ship graffito: A sacred and secular symbol". *The Other Clare*, 35, 39-49.

Loop Head Tourism (www.loophead.ie)

Mayo Ireland (www.mayo-ireland.ie)

Mayo North destined... (www.northmayo.com)

Megalithic Ireland (www.megalithicireland.com)

MET Éireann (www.met.ie)

Mizen Head Signal Station Visitor Centre (www.mizenhead.ie)

Museums of Mayo (www.museumsofmayo.com)

My Inishowen (www.visitinishowen.com)

My Secret Northern Ireland (www.my-secret-northern-ireland.com)

National Parks & Wildlife Service (www.npws.ie)

The New Statesman (www.newstatesman.com)

Office of Public Works (www.opw.ie)

On-line World of Wrestling (www.onlineworldofwrestling.com)

Ordinance Survey Ireland (2012). Official Road Atlas Ireland.

Puck Fair – Ireland's Oldest Fair (www.puckfair.ie)

Rathmullan.net (www.rathmullan.net)

Riley, J. (2003). *Ghosts of Kilrush*. RavensYard Publishing.

Rootsweb (www.rootsweb.ancestry.com)

Rough Guides (www.roughguides.com)

Slieve League Cliffs Centre (www.slieveleaguecliffs.ie)

Sligo Heritage (www.sligoheritage.com)

Smith, M. (2000). *An Unsung Hero*. The Collins Press.

Tarbert Bridewell Courthouse & Jail (www.tarbertbridewell.com)

Teach na Miasa (www.croagh-patrick.com)

The Burren Connect Project (www.burrenconnect.ie)

The Irish Story (www.theirishstory.com)

The Lonely Planet Guide (www.lonelyplanet.com)

The Mayo News (www.mayonews.ie)

The Sacred Island (www.carrowkeel.com)

The Southern Star (www.southernstar.ie)

The World Factbook (www.cia.gov/library/publications/the-world-factbook)

The Yeats Society (www.yeatssociety.com)

Tour Donegal (www.tourdonegal.com)

Visit Buncrana (www.visitbuncrana.com)

Walking and Hiking Ireland (www.walkingandhikingireland.com)

Welcome to Ardfert.com (www.ardfert.com)

Welcome to Erris (www.visiterris.ie)

Welcome to Ballycastle (www.ballycastle.ie)

We Love Donegal (www.welovedonegal.com)

West Cork Travel (www.westcorktravel.com)

West Cork – A Place Apart (www.westcorkplaceapart.com)

Whiddy Island Ferry (www.whiddyislandferry.com)

World Resources Institute (www.wri.org)

INDEX

Index

Index

Index